SO YOU GIRLS REMEMBER THAT

Gaadgas Nora Bellis

with Jenny Nelson

So You Girls Remember That

MEMORIES OF A HAIDA ELDER

**HARBOUR
PUBLISHING**

HARBOUR PUBLISHING CO. LTD.
P.O. Box 219, Madeira Park, BC, VON 2H0
www.harbourpublishing.com

MAPS by Gowgaia Institute
EDITED by Pam Robertson
TEXT DESIGN by Libris Simas Ferraz/Onça Publishing
PRINTED AND BOUND in Canada
PRINTED on paper with 100% recycled content

Harbour Publishing acknowledges the support of the Canada Council for the Arts, the Government of Canada, and the Province of British Columbia through the BC Arts Council.

LIBRARY AND ARCHIVES CANADA CATALOGUING IN PUBLICATION
Title: So you girls remember that : memories of a Haida Elder / Gaadgas Nora Bellis with Jenny Nelson.
Names: Bellis, Gaadgas Nora, author. | Nelson, Jenny, 1947- author.
Description: Includes bibliographical references.
Identifiers: Canadiana (print) 20220151407 | Canadiana (ebook) 20220151539 | ISBN 9781550179774 (softcover) | ISBN 9781550179781 (EPUB)
Subjects: LCSH: Bellis, Gaadgas Nora. | LCSH: Haida Gwaii (B.C.)—Biography. | CSH: First Nations Elders—British Columbia—Haida Gwaii—Biography. | CSH: First Nations women—British Columbia—Haida Gwaii—Biography. | LCGFT: Autobiographies.
Classification: LCC E99.H2 B45 2022 | DDC 971.1/1200497280092—dc23

On behalf of Nora, Charlie, Maureen and Jenny,
To Nora's family,
To the Yahgu 'laanaas clan,
To the families of Old Massett and Skidegate,
To the people of Haida Gwaii

Royalties will be donated to the Carl Hart Legacy Trust through the Haida Gwaii Community Foundation, to support the T'aalan Stl'ang Rediscovery wilderness youth camp.

Haida and English place names on the north end of the Haida Gwaii archipelago. The northern island, Graham Island, is the largest. Map by Gowgaia Institute

Table of Contents

Preface

Naanii Nora was a storyteller. She wanted to record her memories for family and friends. She often talked about it, with me, with Maureen, passing conversations. In 1992, at the request of her son Charlie Bellis, we recorded four tapes. I transcribed. Later I worked on the story in bits, as life allowed, patching it into shape through time and place. Meanwhile, Maureen McNamara and Nora were busy. When Maureen died, so young, I received fifteen cassette tapes of their work aimed at a wider audience. They sat in a box, forgotten. Eventually, Charlie and I began the push to finish. I rediscovered Maureen and Nora's tapes and the story suddenly mushroomed.

For my part, I have transcribed, researched, talked with a lot of fine people, and put the whole into roughly chronological order. These are Nora's words, excerpted from the cassette tapes, collated into stories and sorted into time and place. Gesture, tone, rhythm or meaning may be misread or lost by putting voice into print. Just moving a comma can alter meaning. Occasionally I have added words, in square brackets, to clarify meaning but stay true to her voice. I have tried to be meticulous, check carefully, and share Nora's story with family and Elders. The responsibility for any error in transcription or research is mine.

Nora's story is arranged in chapters: Nora and her family, memories of childhood, seasonal stories of people and place, song and meaning, the 1910s and 1920s, Nora's move to New Masset, marriage, widowhood and reflections. The villages of Old Massett, the ancient

Haida community, and Masset, the nearby settlement town, are referred to as they were at the time, as Massett and New Masset.

Charlie wanted to weave in the history of the Haida political relationship with Canada. For Maureen, the Haida social and cultural values expressed by Nora through her life were so important. She wanted this book to express "Nora's spirit of living—her joy, humour, spirituality and gentle power, resourcefulness, love of children, love of music and social life, kindness, strong will, creativity… the spirit that nurtures and endures."

As in all good stories, Naanii Nora's story is larger than herself. It is a story of her times, and part of the Haida tale.

Maureen died in Masset on August 19, 1995. Nora died on May 6, 1997, in long-term care in Queen Charlotte City Hospital. Charlie died at home on a fine morning in May 2003. So.

—Jenny Nelson

Naanii Nora and friends at Dockside Charlie's circa 1994 (*around the table*): Claude Savard, Nora, Vicki Bragan, Jenny Nelson and Jaalen Edenshaw, with Sophie and Sluuguu.
Collection of the author

Orthography

I am not a linguist. Charlie directed me to Naanii Mary Swanson for language. The spelling conventions used to represent Haida words were chosen in consultation with Naanii Mary, Marianne Boelscher Ignace and those currently working to develop Haida orthography in Old Massett. I am grateful to Marianne for her research, for answering so many questions, and for edits and linguistic notes.

In Old Massett there are several dialects of the Haida language with different spellings. Standardized spelling is evolving, and the spellings used herein reflect current usage to the best of my knowledge.

For the English meaning of Haida names, as the basis of the family trees, and for additional insights I have referred to John Enrico's valuable 1991 work entitled "Draft on Names" and his family tree research for Old Massett in the 1990s. Note that John Enrico did years of research and publishing after that work, and that this information does not necessarily reflect his later understandings of the language.

Marianne Boelscher Ignace edited the manuscript of this book for X̲aad Kil—for Haida language spelling, meaning and context—and provided the pronunciation guide below. I am in her debt. Haw'aa. As was the preference of X̲aad Kil learners in Old Massett at the time of final editing, X̲aad Kil words are rendered in the practical Alaskan orthography. Spelling variations exist and have occurred over time, which is reflected in the maps and material from outside sources.

Since Nora spoke mostly English, place names are usually the English names, as Nora spoke them.

PRONUNCIATION GUIDE

MASSETT HAIDA VOWELS:
The short *a* vowel sounds like the vowel in "sun."
The long *aa* vowel sounds like the *a* in "father."
The *i* sounds like the short *i* in "pin."
The long *ii* sounds like *ea* in "bean" or *ee* in "been."
The short *u* sounds like the *u* in "put."
The long *uu* sounds like the *oo* in "moon."
The ending *gee* or *ee* in Massett sounds like the *ay* in "may."

MASSETT HAIDA CONSONANTS THAT DON'T OCCUR IN ENGLISH:
G̲ is pronounced deep in the throat, almost like a glottal stop.
X (without underline) sounds like a strong *H* made in the mouth
 (like German word "ich").
X̲ (with underline) sounds like a strong *H* made in the throat
 (like German word "loch").
The *k̲* is a "throat *k*" made further down in the throat than the regular
 k sound.
The *hl* is like a voiceless *l*: tongue against the roof of your mouth;
 blow out through the sides.
In addition, X̲aad Kil has some "pinched" or glottalized sounds,
 like *k'*, *k̲'*, *t'*, *tl'*, *p'* and *ts'*; these "ejective" sounds are made by
 closing your throat for an instant, and then forcing air out as
 you say the sound.

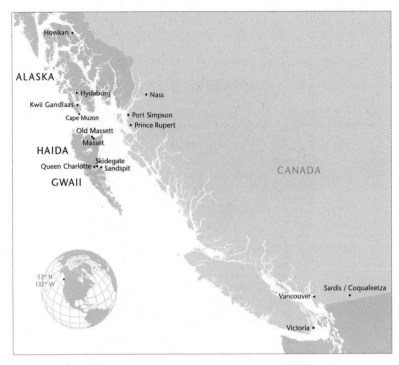

Haida Gwaii is the ancient home of the Haida. The remote archipelago off the northern coast of British Columbia is eight hours by ferry from Prince Rupert on the mainland. Victoria, the province's capital, is 750 miles to the south. Map by Gowgaia Institute

Naanii Nora in her ceremonial Haida regalia. Roberta Lynn Aiken photo, Byrds Eye View Photography

CHAPTER 1

So you girls remember that

NAANII NORA

My name is Gaadgas. Haida name.
When you pan gold, it makes noise.
The bottom of the pan sounds heavy.
They said, "guud gas."

Guudgas,[1] short for Guud gaadgas.
Moses say it means when they pan for gold.
If it's gold it's heavier. It makes a different sound.
It sound heavier in the bottom of the pan.
So they get the name Gaadgas.

Pure gold in the bottom of the pan.
So my name is Pure Gold.
Amen.

Maureen McNamara picking huckleberries at North Island, July 1990, during the Haida-led blockade of the sports fishery. Lisa Gordon photo

Nora's son Charlie Bellis, aboard his boat, the *Lady Julia*. Donated by Margo Hearne

CHARLIE AND MAUREEN

> *"I can write all those things down, but I can't. I haven't got the help to write all these things down. Lots of people would like to know. We talk about all these things. You must remember them. You win a prize for it."*
> —Nora, laughing, to Maureen

1984

Visiting Naanii Nora is one of my pleasures. Down the lane beside her son's house, up the steps past the woodshed to her door. Fixed to the door is a mousetrap for messages.

Nora is sitting by her wood cookstove crocheting a red wool tam. Buns are baking in the oven; family photos hang on the wall. Dangling from the overhead light cord within easy reach is a brown plastic 'Indian' chief.

Nora's face lights up for a visitor. "Oh goody. Sit down. Do you want a cup of tea?"

I look around for a place to sit. There are empty tin cans and bags of wool, jars of guitar screws and buttons and nails, bags of clothes, a sewing machine, a drum, two guitars to be mended, an accordion, dried fish. Nora is getting deafer these days, but we manage to talk. And there's always something to laugh about, a laugh that stays with me for the rest of the day.

I choose a flowered teacup from her cupboard shelf.

Nora was born in 1902 in Old Massett on Haida Gwaii,[2] at the north end of Graham Island, by the mouth of Masset Inlet. Later she was one of the first Haida to live in New Masset, the new white settlers' town farther up the shore. Her Welsh-Canadian husband died while the children were still young.

Nora's mother Gudaa x̱iigans, Susan Bennett, was a Yahgu 'janaas Raven, family matriarch, gardener, food gatherer, weaver. Her father, Captain Andrew Brown, was a boat builder, storekeeper and argillite carver, a food gatherer

and a storyteller. Nora was the precious darling baby girl, a survivor after a series of sibling deaths, boss of her dad and a gang of younger brothers. Life was so good.

Today I've brought her a few of the first salmonberries, picked on the way over to her house, soft and plump and orange, on a large salmonberry leaf. I sit on an upturned white plastic bucket. Nora serves tea from her table, a two-shelved

Nora at home. Gina Mae Schubert photo

metal cart on wheels, where she keeps things handy: sugar and jam and a can of milk with a golf tee in the hole, her own invention "to keep out the flies," a few jars of nails and pins, a hammer, a hand drill that I covet, a beef bone pencil holder.

Nora has a flair for life and laughter. She has a gift for costume, classy split-second hats and a good punchline. She has a passion for recycling and can probably make anything needful out of a condensed milk can and bits of wire or wool.[3] Before her hands were too weak with age to hold a hammer, Nora was a home handyma'am, musician, barber, baker and tinker, and she is still a patcher.

Nora says, "My grandfather believe in not getting warm up in the old wood that been built for him to come home.

"He has to get fresh limbs, great big limbs, to make great big fire, and then he get himself warm up. He has to go right up to get those limbs. He had to bring them home and then make the fire.

"They poor as long as they live, if they warm themself up in old fire that been built before, while he's out. He believe in that."[4]

My ear delights in the lilt and rhythm of her speech. I reach for a pencil and an empty BC Hydro envelope from the table and start to scribble. Nora's grandfather was Naa ḵajuud, Warms the inside of the house.[5]

MY MOTHER'S NAME WAS SUSAN

"My mother's name was Susan. Gudaa x̱iigans,[6] Something that you love, the one that keeps you company. That's the meaning of it. Real nice name."
—Nora

Gudaa x̱iigans's father was Naa ḵajuud, a Tsiits* git'anee Eagle from Yaan[7] (Yan), his clan originally from up the inlet at Tsiits.

Susan's mother was Gid gudgaang, Chief's daughter whom they think of, of the Yaahl naas Yahgu 'janaas x̱aadee clan. Her maternal grandmother, who died young, was from Ḵwii G̱andlaas,[8] Alaska, part of the Alaskan Haida who had moved to Massett and were close to the G̱aw (Massett) Yahgu 'laanaas.[9]

Gudaa x̱iigans and her siblings were Yahgu 'laanaas Ravens. Diinan River summer camp and a Diinan hunting area passed to her brother Robert. When Massett's first missionary arrived in 1876 he began to replace Haida names with English names. Gudaa x̱iigans's mother, Gid gudgaang, became Annie; and her father, Naa ḵajuud, was renamed John Luke Bennett.

There were five children. Gudaa x̱iigans (Susan) was the eldest, probably born in 1873,[10] followed by Kwah i'waans, Big blowing of killer whale (Benjamin), in 1874, Kliijuuklaas[11] (John Luke) in 1875, Kwahsaas, Breaching seaward (Robert), in 1876, and Ḵ'ii 'iljuus, Viewed as power-ful (Lydia), born in 1890.[12] Another brother, Skil ḵiiyaas, Light wealth spirit (perhaps William), drowned at sea.

This is Nora's mother Gudaa x̱iigans, Susan Brown, in 1947. She was born into the Yahgu 'laanaas Raven clan. Marius Barbeau photo, Canadian Museum of History, CD1996-1151-009

In the 1890s, Naa ḵajuud erected a bear pole,[13] perhaps the last memorial pole to be raised in Massett for the next eighty years.

---

* Tsiij is the official Haida Nation spelling, but in conference with Massett speakers, they preferred Tsiits.

Gudaa x̱iigans died at home. She was buried March 13, 1958. Charlie remembered watching his grandparents rowing up the inlet shortly before her death.

CAPTAIN ANDREW BROWN

"Oh, I love my dad so much."
—Nora

Nora's father, Duuan 'iljuus,[14] Noble younger brother, was an Eagle of the Tsiits git'anee. His birthdate is uncertain,[15] but he may have been born shortly after the 1862 smallpox epidemic. There is record of his having two sisters, X̱ahl gunjuus,[16] Shiny cute little thing (Eliza), born in 1861, and Kil t'aawee, Copper voice (Gertie). Nora said, "They think so much of him because he's the only brother."

He was known as Captain Andrew Brown. His mother was a Tsiits git'anee Eagle, Esther Sdahl k̲'awaas.[17] Her family Chief was Sdiihldaa (Returned) of the Git'ans Eagles from Yan.[18]

Duuan 'iljuus's father, a Massett argillite carver and canoe maker, was Walter Kingaagwaaw, Refusing-the-news,[19] a Raven from Yan. His clan was Stl'ang 'laanaas[20] (Rear Town People), originally from the Nee kun (Naikoon) village near Rose Spit. Esther and Walter's marriage on May 7, 1887, was recorded at St. John's Anglican Church: "Walter Kingagwo 41 and Esther StehlthKouwas 29 married according to Indian custom, parents Yelthou, deceased and Daien, deceased."[21]

Kingaagwaaw's older stepbrother, also a carver, was John Gwaay t'iihld, Wets the island.[22] He died in 1912, at about ninety years old. According to Robin Wright, John Gwaay t'iihld was one of two who carved many of the totem poles at Yan.[23] His tombstone, with a Raven-finned killer whale design by Charles Edenshaw, is in the Old Massett cemetery.[24]

Kingaagwaaw's stepfather's name was Yaahl naaw (Raven House), of the Ḡaw Stl'ang 'laanaas.[25] Both brothers portrayed Haida peoples out of daily life, Kingaagwaaw in argillite, Gwaay t'iihld in wood. Barbeau noted, "their statuettes and high reliefs rank with the best in Haida art."[26]

Andrew Brown told Barbeau that his grandfather was Chief of Nasduu (Hippa Island), where he owned beachcombing rights: "When a whale was stranded there along a coast-line of forty miles, it was my grandfather's property. Beyond this limit, it belonged to other chiefs."[27] His village was Ḡat'anaas ("Bilge-water-town") on Nasduu.

Nora's father, Duuan 'iljuus, Captain Andrew Brown, was a renowned boat builder and argillite carver. Marius Barbeau photo, Canadian Museum of History, CD1996-1151-006

Captain Andrew Brown died at home, January 18, 1962. His obituary appeared in *The Native Voice* the following month, reading in part: "Famed patriarch of the Haida Indians, noted totem pole carver and one of the first Native boat builders on the Pacific Coast, Capt. Andrew Brown died in Masset on January 18. Reported to have been born before the coming of the first Anglican missionaries. The date of Capt. Brown's birth is not known. He was believed to be in the vicinity of 100 years old….

"He was best known in recent years for his beautiful slate totem poles which he carved for many years. A student of history, he was also rich in the knowledge of Haida legends."

CHAPTER 2

Massett

Alfred Adams, Massett:

"Making large canoes was a steady income for the Haidas: they made them for the Stikine, the Skeena, the HB Co. [Hudson's Bay Company]."[28]

Newton H. Chittenden, 1884:

"Massett is the shipyard of the Hydas, the best canoe makers on the continent, who supply them to the other coast tribes. Here may be seen in all stages of construction these canoes which, when completed, are such perfect models for service and of beauty."[29]

In the late 1870s Massett was a vibrant hub of Haida society and a canoe building centre.
O.C. Hastings photo, 1879, Royal BC Museum and Archives, PN10980

George A. Dorsey:

George Dorsey visited Massett one May, sometime in the 1870s. He was twenty-six hours in a boat in sight of Tow Hill, caught in a gale and the current, waves washing over them every few minutes. The next day was calmer: *"...a favorable tide bears us rapidly down the inlet; a minute more and we sight Masset—a strange, quaint little sleepy village, with its tall totem poles and row of cottages.... Masset is the Clyde of the coast, and in the fall and winter the little street along the water's edge is lined with great cedar logs, which are being chipped, steamed, pressed, and fashioned into canoes, some over fifty feet long."[30]*

The house of Chief Henry Weah, Old Massett, circa 1879. Fish dry on a rack to the right. The large house was built circa 1940. In *The Queen Charlotte Islands, 1774–1966, Volume I,* Kathleen E. Dalzell identifies those out front (*left to right*): "Wm. Harding, Joshua Collison, Mathew Skil-tling (father of Wm. Matthews, Chief Weah today), Wm. Matthews (boy), Mr. R. Dodd (H.B.C.), Alexander McKenzie, retired H.B.C., Henry Edenshaw and Reuben Thompson. Lady seated to right of door was Mr. Wm. Matthews' mother. Lady in white scarf was the first wife of Chief Henry Weah." Photographer unknown, probably O.C. Hastings, Royal BC Museum and Archives, PN05339

MASSETT 1876

Cold ocean waters rush out of the north Pacific into a long inlet. To the east near the inlet mouth a distant line of poles stand dark against a dull winter sky. Ḡad Ḡaywaas.

Smoke floats out of roof holes from Ḡad Ḡaywaas, from lits'aaw where houses cluster on the hill, and farther south down the shore, from K̲'aayang. Northwest across the inlet, smoke rises from twenty hearth fires at Yaan.*

On shore a wave breaks, rattling the stones. Rising from tall beach grass, cedar eagles and ravens and bears, the story keepers, watch the inlet from their places on the crest poles.

A wide footpath runs between the houses and the shore. Village houses, long and low with massive cedar beams and corner posts, crowd together facing the sea. Some have a carved frontal pole standing forty to fifty feet high, gyaa'aang, with an entrance hole in the centre. Inside, the floor descends in tiers to the hearth-fire. Behind the homes are grave-houses, muskeg and forest.

Everyone crowds to shore to watch the steamer arrive, joking, greeting visitors and friends, unloading freight.

The steamship *Otter* has recently begun to stop at Massett twice a year, in the spring with Hudson's Bay Company store supplies, and in the fall to take away trade goods, wood and stone carvings, silver jewelry, fur seal and otter pelts, dogfish and seal oil, potatoes. A few years ago, after lengthy deliberation, villagers had permitted an elderly white man, Martin H. Offutt, with his Tsimshian wife and family, to set up the Hudson's Bay Company store and post office in Massett.[31] At the end of the year another white man, his wife and

---

* A fourth community is sometimes mentioned—Ts'aagwaal, from the word *fern*, between lits'aaw and K̲'aayang.

After the epidemics of the 1800s, people from these old Haida towns along the north and west sides moved to Massett—into the four constituent towns of Ḡad Ḡaywaas, Iijaaw, Ts'agwaals and Ḵa'aayang. Map by Gowgaia Institute

young son, arrive by steamer. It is William Henry Collison, Massett's first missionary. An unused longhouse becomes the first church.

It was just fourteen years ago that the last smallpox epidemic ravaged the Haida people.[32] Remnants of peoples from the northern coastal and inlet villages, the survivors, have gradually moved into Massett, the people from Tiiaan, Tliiduu, Yaaku, K'yuust'aa (Kiusta), Ts'aa.ahl, Daadans, Ḵang, Ya'aats', Kuneelang, Hl'yaalang (Hiellen), Nee kun (Naikoon), Yaagan kun, Yaakun, Tsiits, Juus ḵaahlii (Juskatla), and later, Yaan.[33]

Villagers at Yan pose for the camera in front of Flicker House and a memorial pole to a chief of the Tsiits Town Eagles, 1881. The pole had an eagle on top, nine potlatch rings and a hummingbird at its base. Nora's family moved from Yan to Massett. Her grandmother still gardened at Yan. Andrew Brown grew up there before the first missionary came. Edward Dossetter photo, American Museum of Natural History, 32959

The pace of village life moves with tide and season. There is a time for fur seal hunts, for canoe trips to the mainland to trade, for gardening, fishing, hunting, gathering, weaving and carving, a time for social events and political debate. In fall and winter, the village shore is alive with canoe making. Huge logs, shaped deep in cedar stands further up the inlet, rest on shore. Ravens and crows are noisy, watching men walk down to the beach to work on a canoe.[34]

Children play nearby. Nora's mother, Gudaa x̱iigans, is three years old.

Six years later, the people of Massett return from the summer fishing grounds and canneries to find that Reserve Commissioner Peter O'Reilly had visited Massett to set the first Haida reserves.[35]

By the 1890s, the last totem pole has been raised and some poles have been felled. A few longhouses lie open to the weather, replaced by smaller, European-style houses.

Marriages are still arranged by parents. On January 5, 1890, Nora's father and mother, Duuan 'iljuus and Gudaa x̲iigans, are married in Massett. They are recorded in the church records as Andrew Duanelyus and Kwutahegins, ages twenty and seventeen.[36] Their fathers, Kingaagwaaw and Naa k̲ajuud, are documented as Albert Kinagwo and John Nakadyut, both canoe makers from Massett. Missionary Charles Harrison marries the two in the new church, St. John's Anglican. The original mission house had burned.

The other main village is the Haida town of Skidegate, reached by foot inland from the bottom of Masset Inlet, or by boat 120 miles along an often perilous east coast. It is 1900. The missionary in Massett is now Reverend Will Collison, son of Reverend William Henry Collison, and he is accompanied by his sister Emily.[37]

Ex-missionary Charles Harrison is now revenue collector for Massett, with a cattle ranch north of the village along the Dal k̲aahlii (Delkatla) estuary and ambitions to create a settlement nearby.

By the time Nora is born, her mother has given birth to seven or eight children. At least three died within their first weeks, and three within a few years of Nora's birth. Only the first born, Eliza, has survived.[38]

Nora is born in a house at G̲ad G̲aywaas, just north of the hill. At the back of the house is a large lean-to off the kitchen where Andrew and Susan have a store. The house smells of dried fish and wood smoke. Evenings, you might hear the sound of singing and drumming and laughter spill out onto the roadway from the house.

It's mid-October 1902, and the moon is shining on the inlet and the small village spread along the shore.

CHAPTER 3

Jacob's Ladder

My mother said when I was born, there's a window. She said that a real bright light shone right on my small face, just round. I was laying there by Mom. And she look up, and here it's right from the moon. It shone right on my face when I was just born. Later on she thought it was something real wonderful. "Right straight down on the baby's face," she said. We call it Jacob's Ladder.* So she think, "Something special. You might be born for something good." Well, it's in my mind.

MY GRANDPARENTS

My grandparents lived little ways from us, right behind that [community] hall, the one burned down, underneath the hill. They living alone. These days the grandmothers raise the grandchildren. Not those days at all. I could see [visit] them. They always be alone. They living alone. I used to help my grandmother with everything. Of course I like to help other people, since I was kid.

I think her name was Annie. Her Haida name is Gid gudgaang. It means that you feel like a real precious girl. She feel like a real little darling—that's what it means. She felt that way, real precious.

---

* Jacob's Ladder: Genesis 28:10–15.

My grandfather's name was Luke Bennett. They're from—I remember they always talk about Yan. They said my grandfather was real good canoe builder.

My grandfather was blind, went blind in 1901. He got hit on the sail. There's a big lumber sailing boat, like—the bottom was that big. When it's rough that sail thing blewed over and hit him on the head. He went blind right after that. Right here [back of head] it's real bad if you got bumped. It's mucked up inside there I guess. So he was blind since I can remember. My grandmother look after him all the time I remember it. Cook for her husband.

They used to go across there to Yan to live there for holiday out of town. They built a big house across there. Now there's no house left. My grandmother always take me away from my mother when they go out camping.

I was born 1902. Mother said that's the time one of my uncle got drowned out here from my dad's schooner, out in the mouth of the Masset Inlet. They cause a great big trouble amongst my uncle and my granny and my grandfather and my dad. They were mad at my dad for building boat.

I think his name was William. I don't know. It was so long. I know his Haida name though. His name was Skil ḵiiyaas.[39] And they didn't find his body even. So when I was born it was tough time because mother feel too hurt. He's her own brother. So.

Real sad winter for my mother. And more like I had a real tough time when I was baby and my mother don't nurse me. She just raise me in oatmeal. No milk. She was too sick, too worry. She can't nurse me.

I raised on porridge since I was a baby, and now I start eating it again.

I got the oldest, oldest grandparents in Massett. They live long time. They're real old when they die. She died real old. She running around getting things at Yan village and she fell down and she didn't get up.

My grandfather start to grow new teeth, when he died, a small little teeth, just like a baby's teeth. That's how old he was. Real old man.

SKIL K̲IIYAAS

The death of Skil k̲iiyaas at sea is still remembered by the family. Luke's sister, the late Lucy Frank, told this to her son, the late Moses Ingram. It is passed to us by Nora's cousin, the late Claude Jones.

Claude Jones:
"They lived at Yan. His mother told everyone, 'Get ready. Get dressed. There's going to be some bad news coming over to us.' Sure enough, people came and said her son was lost off a schooner at the bar [sandbar].

"His mother used to go down to the rocks. A killer whale would come up, rest its head up on the rocks, and she'd sit there and talk to it. She believed that it was her son that she lost. They'd cook fish and she'd bring it a drink of water."[40]

When her grandmother died at Yan, Nora's younger cousin, Connie, was barefoot with her mother in their garden near 7-Mile, where her paternal grandfather Skil kwiitlaas (James Jones) had a garden. They heard three shots. Three shots meant bad news. Her mother Lydia lifted her up on her back and carried her down to the boat.

Connie remembered that in Massett, all of her grandmother's things were laid out in the house with the body in the traditional way, and how much she wanted the blue and red beads there.[41]

Claude Jones:

"Luke Bennett died with a third set of baby teeth, when he was 125 years old, near as anyone could guess. He was from Juskatla—Tsiits. He was my dad's [Elijah Jones's] uncle. He lived behind where Myron's living, next door to Ernie Yeltatzie and Carrie Weir. He was Emily Thompson's uncle. He died in 1930. The last thing he asked for was his pipe. Robert filled the pipe, lit it, and put it in his mouth. Few minutes later, he died."

SUCH A LARGE FAMILY

Claude Jones:

"Such a large family. So many died. In the 1930s lots passed away, double funerals…

"Them days there was none [no money]. We gathered a lot of food. We didn't need much money. Them days everyone depended on fishing for their livelihood. A lot of people had their own trolling boats, build their own homes. If you didn't own your own house, you couldn't be on the band council. If you can't put a roof over your own head, how can you look after someone else's welfare?

"Those days the chief was chosen from the day you were born. If your uncle didn't choose you, you couldn't get that name.

"Robert Bennett—his name was given by his uncle; the one that lived on top of Iits'aaw.[42] *He was so damned old-fashioned. We were fishing Cumshewa. He had a boat,* Dawn Marie, *which he gave to me down there. He quit. I couldn't take the boat, 'cause it didn't seem right. Wilfred had worked so hard on that boat. Later he wouldn't sell it to me. He passed his name to Eli [Abrahams].*

"John Bennett was married to Reuben Samuels's mother first. They had a fight at Naden Harbour. Her family all got involved in it. He left. Ben [Bennett] saw his fire across the inlet, went up the hill and called his brother. They went across to get him. John went to Alaska. He signed

According to Claude Jones, this Bennett family photograph includes (*left to right*): (*back*) Robert Bennett, Ben Bennett, (*middle*) Julia Bennett, Luke Bennett, Susan Brown, (*front*) Lydia Jones with baby James, Eliza Abrahams. "Robert is the younger man—six feet tall. Ben is standing on the steps." Image courtesy of the Bellis family

some papers for divorce. He discovered years later that he had signed citizenship papers.

"Ben—he always tell people when they brought the water in—nobody else supposed to drink before him. I fished with Ben.

"Percy took over where old Ben lived. He chose my oldest brother to pass on to, because James was a good hustler. Susan squawked and instead it went to Percy. Ben never got a tombstone, just as he'd predicted."*

---

* Robert, John and Ben Bennett were Susan's brothers; Percy was Nora's brother.

THE BANDLEADER

I just had five brothers and one older sister. Eliza—she's the oldest one and I got lots of other brothers between. Archie, Percy, Oley, Fritz, Ezra—we call him Smiijuu,[43] that's Small little one.

I got one sister little older than me. She got hurt on her backbone and broke it. Mother said it was just me about, two years old. I just run around. My sister had a little small rocking chair. She's going to sit down. I pulled it away and she fell and broke her. That's what mother said. But I heard it different from Connie, my own cousin.

She said my grandmother always take me away from my mother and go camping, when they go out camping. She used to just come in and take me away across there [to Yan] when I was just baby and both of us and that's the way my sister got hurt. That's what Connie said. But my mother blame me for it. I might of but I don't know. I was too little.

Mother said there's two died when I was a kid, just when I was a baby too. Somebody's giving a dinner and they borrow all mother's table and chairs. My brother wouldn't sit down on the floor. He want to sit down on the table, so mother put him on the table. He fell off and hit back of his head. He went blind right away. Just a tiny, little boy. I think they used to call him Robert. Mother never forgive those people who borrow the chair.

I'm the only one left of a big family. Real hard when you get left alone after you had so many brothers.

I haven't got any girls around close, so it was just one girl I used to play with, Violet Marks's sister—Isabella her name was. I used to love her so much. And we let Solomon Russ, that's her brother, we used to let him be the father for our dolls. I remember it so well.[44]

Connie Webb's mother get a doll for me. Japanese doll. The head was made out of china. She must have find the head and put the body on for me. I was going to trade the doll for an umbrella one time and mother get mad at me. I want umbrella so bad.

The children are out hunting all the time. Summertime, they go out hunting, fishing. When I was kid that's all they used to do.

So I was the only girl amongst the boys and I'm more like a tomboy.[45] I want to play with guns and things like that. I played ball and climbing trees. I rather play with bow and arrow than play dolls. Pretend to be real tough.

My mother said I used to sing all the time. I learn some Indian song, make my brother dancing. I was so darn naughty. If I learned a song, the tune, put all kinds of words in it. I was the leader for my two or three brothers. I keep the band.

My mother used to call me the bandleader. She said I didn't stop singing till I get to know the tune. When they were out hunting for fur seal in those big canoes,[46] I was in the bow—had my three brothers, teaching them how to sing. I was bossing them so much. "Aa ay ii aa" this way, this way, this way, I'm bossing them so much and they listen to me too, mother said. All day long I was singing. About evening time I was dead tired.

GUDAA X̱IIGANS

Mother had small hands, tattoos all up arms, blue. I think Dad had a tattoo on his chest.[47] So much big, when they do that. When they teenagers, maybe.

Captain Andrew Brown:
"I have my crest, an eagle, tattooed on my leg. So have my brothers and sisters. The operation lasted ninety days and cost eight hundred

blankets a day. We lay on feather beds. My aunt, whom we paid for the tattooing, prepared the charcoal and the needles (qep, qep, qep) with a clean cloth. She worked the whole day. We were not allowed to eat grease for a month, lest the tattoo marks should not heal properly."[48]

Mother was kind of bossy, but I'm my dad's pet. I lead the boys astray. My dad never used to get mad. Mother used to, but I don't listen to Mother anyway. I never used to do crochet, sewing. Somehow Mother's kind of cranky. I think I was too bad anyway.

That's all I used to do with Mother, pick strawberries, Tsaawan [Chown River], North Beach. We start out early in the morning, hiking out there with Mother. My grandmother used to tell me how to pick the strawberries. Start from down the beach and go up this way, pick all those and then go back again as it's getting hotter and hotter. Underneath the trees, they're bigger, with the moss—real clean.

Before me, they used to dry them, but not when I was little. Mother makes strawberry jam, wild ones. No canning. Mother and Mrs. Edenshaw, great big pantry just full of strawberry jam and some others. They fill up that great big pantry.

I used to babysit for Mother all the time. Otherwise I know how to split some fish, if mother show me how to do it. Mother don't let me do it because I was the only girl. They spoil me rotten. I saw other girls do it, splitting for drying them, and I don't know nothing about it. Same way with making weaving. She didn't want me to do it.[49]

All I do since I was grow up I go around play music with some other boys. I rather go out climbing trees with them. I was spoiled rotten. That's why I was real poor housekeeper.

I used to help Mother but Mother was kind of real careful of everything. She like to cook so I don't cook anywhere. But after I was with Fred, that's all I do, cooking. I like to please Mother, do some work, so I grow up with it, doing things for my mother and my dad. I always be around with Dad anyway. The boys are too little and I was tough enough.

I AM THE BOSS

I used to boss my dad all the time. I am the boss. I got two brothers, but I was the one.

[My dad's name was] Duu.un 'iljuus. He call himself Big Eagle in Haida, G̲uud i'waans,[50] but that was his sister's boy's name [Andrew Yorke]. They used to call him Captain Andrew Brown because he earned that name. He built seven big boats. That's why they call him Captain Brown.

You know where he was born? He used to tell us that he was born on the canoe going over to mainland. Great big canoe. He grow up at Yan. And then they move over here when he was teenager, to Massett, when missionary came. Everybody move into Massett then.

He was about fifteen years old when the first missionary came to Massett. They take all the teenagers. They teach them how to sing in the church. They take him; he last only two days and they fired him. He run after the girls so much they kick him out he said. "I'll be real good singer now if they didn't kick me out," he said.

He used to read pretty good. He go to school little while and then he was too bad so they kick him out.

My dad and everyone else used to make big canoes. My dad, my grandfather used to talk about everybody's busy with the building the boat in the town. Everybody's busy building big canoes. [It was] just the only boat. Canoe is the thing they go to Victoria on. Great big canoes, whole pile of people get on, go down too.

Since I was baby I grow up on the schooner. Going back and forth, back and forth with Dad. My dad used to go over to mainland all the time, on a sailing boat. Mother used to go with Dad all the time, when they're going over to mainland. There's Mother, and I got about three or four little brothers. They used to be all come over on all the time.

Every time when Dad go over we had to go with him. It was big enough for everybody sleep on it. I know this here [Hecate Strait] just like first reader book. I was so happy.

Mother was a good sailor. One time Mother was at the wheel and it get rough so quick. Just like *boof!* It get so rough. Mother said she wasn't even scared because she was at the wheel. Dad was looking after other things. They were sailing around, at North Island, around east coast, the mountains right from the water, great steep big rock. They're real dangerous-looking. My mother was at the wheel and she couldn't do a thing. The wind was too strong. The sail is quite wide. They can't turn the wheel and here the wind's taking it, going right against the steep hill in the water with its sails on. A few feet away from them *crash*, the wind hits the steep mountains. This sail turns and go the other way, going to Alaska side. They almost get smashed up. Mother almost cry when she's telling us.

We go everywhere. Even down Victoria where Dad doing things.

They went to theatre and I start to howling my head off. I was "wa-wa-wa" real hard. So the actors stop: "Oh my girl. If you want to take my place you can."

So I was all over the place with Mother and them since I was kid. I was spoiled rotten. Nobody's going to have Dad but me. Around Victoria, Mother and them went to the park.* They said

---

* They went to Beacon Hill Park, which is a large seaside park in Victoria, BC.

they'd bought a new coat for my sister, and I wanted one. I keep crying about it. So they put it on me. I look for a mud puddle. I roll in the mud puddle in park. They just laugh at it later on. They said I put that long coat on, roll myself in the mud puddle.

Here I used to think I never get jealous. When I walk around there, after we grow up, I was so ashamed to look at the water puddle. How crazy I could be.

ALTOGETHER SEVEN HE WORK ON

Queen Charlotte Islander, June 17, 1912:
"Captain Andrew Brown successfully launched his gasoline schooner Annie D on the 5th inst. The vessel is forty feet in length and registers fifteen tons. Built of yellow cedar, and with a 14 h. p. Regal engine, the schooner will be a good addition to the craft plying out of Massett Inlet. Capt. Brown will have the novel experience of commanding a schooner on which the whole of the construction work can be credited to his individual labor."

The minute I step on the schooner I start to threw up. Since I was kid. When we going to go on the schooner, going away across there, my mother used to let us eat nothing but orange. When you get seasick, it real easy to come out and you feel better after, she said. That's the way it was. They're real good for getting seasick. And then later on they find out if you eat lots of seaweed before you get on the boat it's easier to come out.

He build that boat. He go to school for it, take lessons from Howkan, Alaska. He work there, pay for his schooling there. That's the way my dad learned how to be boat builder. He's real good at it too.

Mother was there. I think Florence [Davidson]'s dad carving there too. Making totem poles. He's a good carver. Florence's dad from Skidegate they said.

Maybe just one year I guess, he was working there. I think they come over on a sailing boat. You know, it was just like a dream to me.

I remember just little bit, not too much because I was too young. Every day Dad would take me uptown and buy me a hat. Every day I had another hat on. My mother used to laugh and laugh at it. "Look at that thing up there, with

Captain Andrew Brown holding a half model boat, 1919. Models were usually scaled at ¾ inch to the foot, for building a boat. Harlan Smith photo, Canadian Museum of History, 46672

a new hat again." Me, standing there with another hat, every day.

[Returning from Alaska,] Florence was quite big girl. She was about fifteen, just before she got married. She keep on back and forth on the boat. Her dad said, "What you going to get again Jaad ahl k̲'iiganaa?" That's her Haida name.[51] She would say, "Gilg." That's the round hardtack biscuit, from Alaska. It tasted real good. That's why she climb over everybody. Few minutes after she back again where the biscuits are.

Altogether seven he work on. Great big sailing boat, *Charlotte*,* was wrecked. The frame was down there [the tidal slough at the end of Massett] all this time until just lately.

---

* *The Queen Charlotte* was built in Massett in 1895, and was still registered in Victoria to Andrew Brown in 1916. It was a schooner "glt" (glued laminate wood), measuring 52 x 16 x 5.5 feet. (Source: http://www.halfmoon.ca/boats /boatsTZ.html.)

*

He cut the yellow cedar himself from way up the bushes, up the inlet. He do all those things by hand. He made seven big schooners [boats] after that. I thought he built the boat himself, but it wasn't. Some other boys, like Walter Samuels, all his sisters' sons, helping him.

It's so easy to have it then. In those days they got red cedar boards. They make for anything. Somehow they cut it—stripe them up. It's from the red cedar, see. The oars they built from the red cedar. They make their own oars, and the paddles too.

They chop the trees themselves. [They get them] around the inlet. That's where Port Clements and Yakoun River and Aayan [Ain] River, all that, in that great big lake there, and then the slough runs out. That's where the tide goes out. They fall some trees and they drag it out there. Great big things. Imagine how big—the cedar's that big, right straight.

I saw Dad and them cut one. Somebody standing up and somebody down. You know the saw. Long saw to slice the cedar up. Great big cedar there. They slice them up like, split them, for the boat. Build the boat with boards. Make them about one inch, about six inches boards. So they put them on.

They tow them down [to Massett] on the rowboat. With the tide. With the tide it's real easy. You go by the tide most of the time coming down, drifting real fast on the rowboat, with the log. If they get up early enough to go with the tide, you get down in no time. Later on they go on gas boat. But when I was about eight, they all go on a rowboat.

They used to get logs, red cedar, from—I'm not sure if he's the one cutting it. They wreck up a great big foundation [from a deserted longhouse]. And on the shore there, by hand, they cut the lumber for the boat themself. See how smart they are.

But later on, about 1920, everybody got trolling boats, the size of Charlie Bellis's boat [the *Lady Julia*, a wooden thirty-five-foot troller/gillnetter]. The spring salmon used to be real thick. Some people make quite big money trolling for spring salmon. The ones that could [be] fishermens got a real good gas boats. Massett people can help themself with building things real good.

My dad build smaller boat, gas boat. He call it *Partner*. My *Partner*. I grow up on *Partner*. It was real nice shaped one. I remember it so well.

I remember when I was eight years old he build *Annie D.*, that's Annie Deasy, the Indian agent's wife name. Quite big, seine boat. All these white people work for him, five white mens. I remember Bob Johnson.[52] He's the one work for my dad.

My mother was real hard worker. My mother cook for them and I get so fed up with wash dishes. All my brothers just having good time and I was the only one wash the dishes. I used to call, "Mark, mark," at 12:00 [for lunch]. Marking time.

My brother-in-law, Adam Abrahams, got cases and cases of whiskey. They used to get it from Rupert, not around here. There's no liquor store around here. He put it on. They caught him. So they take the boat away from him.[53] It hurt my feelings. We got real poor with Dad [when he lost the boat].

And later on my dad got a thirty-six-foot. He build a boat for himself to go out fishing. We all go out, the whole pile of them. They even go to Alaska on that. Alaska's only forty miles from here. *Cordelia*, the name of that boat was, after uncle's wife. Big seine boat. Dad was helping them building that boat too. He was quite old. They work on it wintertime. And they got everything finished and they go out seining.

And later on, maybe 1930, everybody got a seine boat, real big boat. My dad got one named *Ruth G.* That's the time *Ruth G.* was built, seine boat, his own. That's the latest one he built. The

Indian agent's daughter name was Ruth, Ruth Gillette. He want my dad's boat name after his daughter.

"Annie D in Commission," *The Massett Leader*, April 10, 1913:

"The gasoline schooner Annie D., which formerly belonged to Andrew Brown of the Masset Indians, will be used during the season as a fishery protection boat."

Percy Brown:

Nora's brother Percy helped his father at boat building, their last one being the *Ruth G.*: *"We cut up the ribs by hand. Archie my brother stand above, take us whole week to do it, and then the 2 x 4's another week. Old man marked the boards out and we cut them. We worked like a bugger, six months it took us.*

"Ribs were yellow cedar. We got the ribs at Dinan Bay, on the right hand side, not very far up. Bow stem we got in Hippa, from Skelu—send it home with Tommy Smith. We got the keel of hemlock up at the end of the village, cut the keel right there with broadaxe. You got to know how to use broadaxe, otherwise trim your foot off. I saved up $500 for fir planking, edge grain. Me and my brother caulked it. We never pumped that boat for ten, twenty years. We used oakum, two bales of it, pitch for seams.

"We named her Ruth G. *We bought the name from Gillette; cost us $25 to get the name. We had 20 Vivian [engine]. Next year Matty Yeomans build the* Chief Weah. *She had 30 HP Corliss, three cylinder, lots of noise for nothing.* Ruth G. *went past her like nothing. Adelaide J. had 30 HP. We used to go by her like nothing. We beat him into town, two hours behind us. Old man George Jones was mad, he sure hate us for it.'"*[54]

A GREAT SEAMAN

Marius Barbeau, *Haida Carvers in Argillite*:

"Andrew Brown (according to [Alfred] Adams) was a wood and argillite carver and one of the best boat-builders on the Islands. He built the Queen Charlotte, *the first schooner at Massett, and he had constructed another elsewhere, which was wrecked on Dundas Island. A relative of Robert Ridley, the carver, Brown took him as a partner in the construction of more schooners (according to Peter Hill, of Massett): 'the* Annie D. *and* Seabird. Seabird *was a wind-jammer; and* Annie D. *was a gas boat. Now he owns the* Ruth G. *'"*[55]

Claude Jones:

"First boats were Columbia River boats, from Skeena gillnetting. Then they start building boats themselves—Robert and Alfred Davidson, Robert and Andrew Williams, Joe and Isaac Edgars, Ed Russ, Louis Bell.

"Boats were built where Samuels's house is. Grass flats used to run away out." He remembers a boat launching: *"They went up and brought down four gallon cans of oolichan oil, dumped it on the runners to pry the boat down to the water. Nass River oolichan grease now costs $80 a gallon.*

"Andrew Brown had a small trolling boat. He gave it to Joshua Abrahams, maybe as payment for his help. The boat went to Jeffrey Smith. I remember him talking about—he got an engine for his small

> Mr. Edmund Jenkins is now the proud possessor of a dainty little dinghy, beautifully built of yellow cedar by Capt. A. Brown of Old Massett. The peculiar turn of speed of this type of craft was fully demonstrated on Sunday morning. When propelled by the vigorous strokes of her owner, she shot swiftly past the Centre, leaving many of the admiring spectators so overcome by astonishment that they entirely forgot to attend divine service.

A new dinghy made by Andrew Brown received a glowing mention in the *Queen Charlotte Islander* on March 11, 1914.
UBC Library Open Collections

*trolling boat. Someone showed them how to stop it and start it. Him
and Mathias Yeomans went to the west coast, trapping. They got the
motor going and just kept going without stopping."*

Albert Dalzell remembered Andrew Brown as "a great seaman." He
recalled one time when all the boats were huddled in Naden Harbour
from a storm, and Andrew was heading out in the boat, bobbing up
and disappearing behind the next wave.

EVERYTHING WAS SO GOOD

Everything was so good. Things are cheap and they live real good.
That was when I was kid, about five. 1910 everything was real
good. Everybody's out at Naden Harbour. There's a crab cannery—
no fish cannery. There's plenty of money for everybody. You buy
lots of things for few dollars.

Other people used to bring halibut in all the time. They know
where to get them. They go out little ways, not too far. Halibut
bed. It's in one great big hole in the bottom they said. The bait
is devil fish, octopus. I saw them. They tied it down on the hook.
And the halibut swallowed, caught right on the mouth.

Some people had a load of halibut. The boat was half full.
Not everybody. Some people know how to. Everything had a trick
for it and they don't tell each other.

I went out with my dad when I was six. Something's jerking
the line. I'm not going to let Dad know that. I was going to pull it
up myself. Here when it come out it was a small halibut. That's
the only one I ever catch. Just a tiny, chicken halibut.

Everything Dad do I have to be there. I love my dad so much.
I didn't want him to work alone. I don't stay home. I go out with
him all the time, anywhere he goes.

He go up to get some wood, I had to go with him. So I know how to row. Real tough one. They used to tow the logs down from up the inlet. Goes with the tide, go easy. They're maybe about twenty miles from here. There's some hills there.

All the logs are so big. They cut them down and trim it off. They cutting them with a hand saw. Long, great big long saw [two-handled crosscut saw] to cut wood with. One on that side, one on this side. And then they brought them [the logs]. They got enough wood for winter, cutting it all the time.

One time we drift away. One of the oars broke. You can't do with one oar because we got a log towing down. The tide was so strong it took us right out. At nighttime too it go. About October I guess. That's why it got down quick.

And then Dad was howling for help. He yell out, "Oo-oo-oo-oo." He said it has to be four calls that he's in trouble. You have to call four times he said. That means we in trouble. People always be out on the road, I guess. If it's one call they don't listen. Four calls is something break down. They know that there's trouble. That's what he knew. Good thing he knew it.

My brother-in-law got a gas boat so they all come out and get us, towed us in. Real cold. I remember my brother-in-law, Eliza's husband, take his sweater off and put it on me. I was just about eight or nine years old. It getting dark right away, see. Instead of me stay home, I had to go. I'm spoiled rotten.

AND HE HAD A STORE TOO

Russell Samuels, 2002:
"He had stores but they kept him broke, too much credit. I think they were too damn kind-hearted. The story is that he built five schooners, one gas-boat and seiner boat, seven houses with stores."

My dad wasn't a good fisherman at all. He's just a carver and a boat builder. And he had a store too. Take the stuff down North Island. He had a little store there.

They had a house and the other room is quite big. It's full of stuff. Dad would go to Victoria, stock up for the store. He brought it home on his boat, sailing boat. He build that boat. The name of that boat was *Sea Bird*. The way Dad used to call it. He couldn't pronounce "bird" right—*Sea Bird*, he pronounce it different. Of course when we're kids we pronounce it just the way he pronounce it.

Dad would always ask me, singing: "What's my little girl want from Victoria?"

Since I know how to talk, I always say: "I want a small pees pot." Pee pot. A small one. To pee in. He did bring one home. It used to be real small like that.

They used to laugh at it all the time. Make me mad when they laughing. Anything I want I had to get because all I do is tell Dad about what I want. All kinds of hats he brings home. Just to bring lots of things for me. Oh I used to love my dad so much.

My dad drink, but he never make a fool out of himself. He always drink navy rum. When he had a store, when he taking a drink, us kids used to hang around him 'cause he hand out candies and anything. I would tell some other kids, "My dad's drinking now," and we went and hang around. Maybe he just want to get rid of us; give us candy anyway. It used to be stick candy, round ones, long ones. It used to be real cheap in those days. We got away with lots of them.

CANNED STUFF

Before he build a boat, he used to build bed and any furniture. That was before I was born though. He never keep still. He work all the time. And then later on he start to carving some totem poles. So he's a boat builder and he carve totem poles.

I want to get hold of those knifes so bad when I was a kid.

He's the best carver. That's what Moses said. He said, "Why I know he's the best one is, totem poles seven inches long—there's an Indian in the bottom and this man just sitting there, singing away, the tongue inside, the teeth is just perfect; the lips is just perfect."

Dad sure always make lots of money. He's money-maker. Pile of totem poles. That black slate. And he used to go away with it, and make piles of money, come back. And he would bring some broken ones back. He patch them.

And they used to want great big ones. Many times these too big ones are broke. Then he had to patch them up. Just like he guarantee that, [against] breaking of things. Here he make big ones, it's all broken to pieces. You can't even see where he mend it, glued together. Somebody asked him, "How you glue together you can't see?"

"That's easy," he said. "Just put the black slate onto a fire, real fine fire. Grind the black slate, make it powder. And then mix it with the glue and stick it in there." See how smart he was? They couldn't even see where it glued together.

When I grow up, I said, "Dad, don't you make those big ones. It so hard to pack it to Rupert. If they want totem poles, then use empty can of milk. Just fit in empty milk can, and then when you open one side, pack it with paper so it's easier. You can throw it around, in a suitcase. It don't break that way. You save lots of trouble.

Canned stuff—Dad always talk about it. That's my idea. I like to use cans since I was small. I still using it, empty cans.

CARVER AND CRAFTSMAN

Marius Barbeau:
"'Captain' Andrew Brown, an 'Eagle-Man', was one of the early members of a small group of craftsmen who came under the then prevailing influence of Charlie Edenshaw. He was still an active carver in 1939 (at 73 years of age), although his work lacked finish and precision because of his failing eye-sight. He seemed as buoyant and confident as he was during his rambling career on his island, at Vancouver, in Alaska, and at other places.... He occasionally made large totems. For instance, around 1920, at New Westminster he carved a pole about forty feet high....

"His production at its best came too late to be well represented in museum collections, and it is difficult to estimate his talent as a carver of argillite. Yet the Frog, 3 1/2 inches high, with abalone shell eyes, made by him before 1925... is realistic, yet well stylized, and is of fine quality."[56]

Claude Jones:
"He's one of the few carvers of argillite. Welfare would be the last thing he'd ever take. He was a proud old man."

Claude Davidson:
"I think my dad was urged on by Andrew Brown to learn how to carve because he says there's good money in it. Like my dad, he was a boat builder and house builder and carpenter, and could do practically anything, so Andrew Brown told him, 'You better start carving.' In 1944 we went up the Slatechuck to pack argillite for my dad—my brother Alfred, Paul Hill, myself, who else?—five of us, anyway, and Dad came up. I

think he was about sixty years old when we first went up Slatechuck. Old as he was, he went up there with us. The road wasn't too bad then because logging was taking place at that time. After so many years that Dad had this argillite buried, Andrew Brown kept asking him, 'Why don't you start carving?' Finally Dad went to see what kinds of tools he was using. Dad decided to make his own tools, by hand, and then he started carving. Andrew Brown himself carved until about two years before he died."[57]

Kirk Thorgeirson:

Although crab was not a traditionally carved figure, Andrew Brown carved a pole for Eugene Simpson, the year that he started the first crab cannery in Canada, in Naden Harbour. The story is retold by Simpson's great-grandson, Kirk Thorgeirson: *"The story of how the Dungeness crab came to Naden Harbour is somewhat told like this. A boy of the Eagle clan in Skidegate fought the giant halibut and killed it. The boy skinned the halibut and crawled inside and swam to Naden Harbour where a giant crab lived. The battle was fierce but the boy won and chewed up the crab and that is how there are crabs at Naden. This story was told to me by Charlie Bellis. The lady on the bottom of the pole is powerful Dogfish woman. The pole is signed on the bottom with the date 1919. Grandson Gene Simpson now has the pole."*

Andrew Brown carving an argillite pole at his workspace in his Massett house. Isabel Moore photo, Haida Gwaii Museum, Ph03847

MY DAD WAS A STORYTELLER

My dad was a storyteller. He make everybody laugh all the time in a big gathering. They keep on clapping, more, more. He's the funniest man.

In Victoria there's a big banquet and they ask him to sing a love song. He said, "All right." When he started, everybody listening away.

> Hi diddle diddle,
> the cat and the fiddle,
> the cow jumped over the moon.
> The little dog laugh, ha-ha, to see such a sport
> and the dish ran away with his wife.

He used to put more to it to make it real funny. He said that was Haida love song. They said people, big shots, they couldn't stop laughing.

My dad tell story when I was little girl. When I was quite old, he tell the story just the way we used to heard when we were kids. My dad never forget one word out. Just like if he had the book. He never used to change the story, all the same story for ages. How can he remember it? I want to know. Since I was a little girl till I grow up. He still got the same story.

I can't do that. Same words, same story.

Nothing was different, all the stories that he told. The same, since I was kid. I used to listen to him, and listen to his songs. I used to know lots of songs, but kind of forget it now. He sing a song all the time and drum too. Drum with it.

Dad always speaks in a crowd, jokes, make everybody laugh. He's a carpenter, so he knows how to tell story. When he telling story, the songs have to go with it. He don't believe in it when anybody telling story and they didn't put the song with it. "It has to go with it," he said. That's my dad.

And if you in a crowd, don't tell your jokes first thing you get up. You have to wait till the end, it don't spoil your speech. Don't say anything funny at first. Very wise words, not too long at first. And then telling jokes to make people laugh. It's real true.

But Dad said the song has to go with it. And you pick out the song for the things going on, pick out the song for that purpose, not any old way. Like if the teacher doing something—"I got a song for that."

He always sing for my mother, always sing love song. They laugh so much.

> Darling I am growing old
> Silver threads amongst the gold.

That's his love song for my mother. And they always spoil it for him because they laugh so much. Amanda [Edgars] and them calls it "my uncle's love song."

My dad used to play fiddle. My mother said he used to play violin for square dances when they were young. There's going to be dance so he just go around and play the fiddle on the road. When he's coming back, front of the houses. Everybody going crazy they said, all the young girls. Everybody go where they going to play it. My mother said she was just crazy over dances. She's a good dancer too. Square dance.

My dad never was cranky. He gets everything for me. That's why I play all those things. Soon as I want something, used to get it for me. I was spoiled rotten. That's how I play music. I want a piano; Dad got me a piano. I've been playing since about seven years old I guess.

ELIZA

Eliza, she used to be so funny. She think of funny things to say and she used to blame herself. My dad used to say, it's yourself doing it, even when other people do that [Eliza copying her dad].

My mother said Eliza was real bad when she was kid. Mother talk cranky, "Sweep the floor." Eliza started. Soon's somebody come for her, she just threw the broom down, way she ran away. That's the part my mother always tell me about. She used to be real bad. She didn't care. She just threw the broom down, right on the floor, and way she ran away.

She's the one look after me so much and when I was baby. And I got scabby all over one time, she said. Eliza feel sorry for me and she keep on kissing it. Next thing her face is all scabby.

Eliza Abrahams and Maggie Weir in Massett. Haida Gwaii Museum, Ph03131

See that's contagious hey. I don't know what it was, but they said my face was all scabby. Next thing Eliza's was all scabby.

Eliza was allergic to crab—even if she see it or smell it. Her nose was that big one time, and I couldn't stop laughing. She was mad at me.

Mother and them had a store when I was kid. She didn't go to school but she know how to make change. Mother is working in the store all the time. Just my sister raised me. Eliza. She treat me like her own baby. They used to go over to mainland all the time. Some strangers thought that was her baby that she pack around all the time. She was just a little young girl.

Oh she used to lie to me all the time. One day I came home from school. She always call me "Sister." "Sister, did you hear the news?" she said. "They bring a dead body from Naden."

"Dead body" is k̲'uud. And this man's name was K̲'uud—it's Leila [Abrahams]'s grandfather. The word is k̲'uud. They bring somebody's k̲'uud.

"They brought a dead man's body from Naden Harbour," she said.

"Whose body is that?"

"They brought k̲'uud."

So I run back to the school real fast and here I told the little girls. "They brought K̲'uud's body home from Naden Harbour," I said.

And the relation to this K̲'uud running right to Mother and them's place. She ask Eliza, "Your sister told people in the school that our uncle died in Naden Harbour. She told everybody." Martha Spence said, "Your own sister Nora told my sisters. What she make up that lie for?"

My sister lied to me and I went and spread it. I used to believe everything what she told me.

And Port Simpson, when Dad and them get there on the schooner, there's company store they call it. Great big road goes right underneath the basement. We're sliding down. Oh I had a great big fun. She comes up and "Did you see the cows around here, chasing kids around?" she said. I believe everything what she says. I run and tell all the kids. There was no cows in Port Simpson. She like to lie to me. She always say, "I April fool you." She treat me like a small baby.

She always—if I call Dad, she just kind of move me away and then she call Dad herself. So one time we went up on a boat to Port Clements. I said, "Dad, pass the sugar."

Right away, "Dad pass me the sugar," she said. And Dad wouldn't even listen to me. So I said, "Captain Brown, will you please pass the sugar." And all the boys were with us laughing away. They knew what's going on. She just didn't want somebody else to pay attention to me. Jealous I guess or something like that. I pay her back.

TLIIYAA[58]

I was about five years old, I think. I ran away from the school, playing on the ice. They don't let kids go up to the slough behind the church.

Just to keep us away from where they're skating at the prairie my sister told me. "Don't you dare to go up the lake again. They saw a great big animal last night," she said.

I listen to her.

"Where there's a great big elderberry bush, right underneath, that great big animal lives there," she said. "They seen it. It's shaped like a donkey with red eyes just like fire," she said. "When kids go up there, that great big animal with a great big eyes on, and great big ears on, he run out there to grab the kids when they play on the ice," she said. I believe her so much.

We used to play house, a tea party underneath the house. One day I pack all my small little teacups to have tea party down underneath in the basement. It's quite high basement, about eight feet high, one side all boarded up.

Here I was singing away, taking all the small cups down for other girls to come. I remember it so well. I look up. Looks like something was moving. Great big eyes.

I look. I think of that great big animal Eliza told me about.

I look. And sure enough there's a great big thing with big ears, just the way my sister told me.

I look again. As small as I was, I didn't want them to think I'm a liar, not get people excited.

And I look again. Big red eyes, just the way Eliza told me. And what make me believe was—it's blinking. Great big red eyes just like she said, blinking.

So I just scream and run upstairs. My dad was taking things from the boxes to put them away on shelves in the store. I jump on his shoulders, "I saw Tliiyaa sitting underneath the house!" I was howling my head off.

He want to go down to see it but I wouldn't let him go down. At last he went down and sure enough this thing with red eyes on. It was a great big stump underneath, with roots going up look like ears. And between that there's great big knotholes on the wall.

Sun setting was red and these knotholes on the wall, just on the stump. These big eyes—and blinking, that's what gets me. You know why it's blinking was mother hang some diapers, my mother's clothesline, all the diapers hanging there, blowing away, right on the sunset.

There's no party anymore because there's big Tliiyaa down.

I think they laugh at it all the time, but they don't let me know it. I never go up to the slough again.

I can see it still the way it look because I believe it so much. It sound so true and it *looks* so true too. I thought it was the best thing was ever happened to me.

CHAPTER 4

I remember a little bit

> "More like they used to camping some places, and then move into
> Massett. When the summer's over they used to move back home.
> When all the fishings are over. They quit drying [fish] so they
> move in. I remember a little bit."
> —Nora

I'm sitting close to Nora's stove. The weather is still cold and wet, yet someone has managed to bring in fresh seaweed between squalls. Nora's oven door is open, the seaweed on a cookie sheet crisping. We dip it in butter or oolichan grease and crunch happily. Rain patters the roof. It's a storytelling kind of a day. I imagine old Charlie Thompson, Naanii Dorothy Bell's dad, walking by the Yakoun River barefoot, spearing steelhead for the smokehouse; the late Alfred Young, standing on the spit at the river mouth, singing. The song carries across the inlet to people camped at Ain River.

Claude Jones:
"Go to North Island in April. Come back in August. September moved to Ain River, till maybe November. January, 7-Mile to dry halibut. The only requirement for using the houses was to replace the wood you use, replace the kindling for the next person, fill the water."

Mark Bell to Rolly Williams:
"When the elderberries ripen, start to turn red, that's when sockeye run in Naden Harbour."

Henry Geddes:
"They'd fall big alder into the river and put rocks on it to put it down. Springs would come up. Water would get so black. Alder leaves black under the water. Spring would show up white against the black, and they'd spear them."

Emma Matthews:
"I was born there, at Yakoun. It was 18 something [1894]... And they got a village in Juskatla [Juus ḵaahlii], a big village there and from there they all move around on account of fresh food.

"They got a nice place at the mouth of Juskatla too. And that's where they stay for a while. Lots of big longhouses. The island—Tsiits. That's why the tribe's called Tsiits git'anee today.

"And from there you move to where they plant potatoes and other things. That's Gathlang daangkun. I guess you know where it is, at the mouth of Yakoun River. And at Yakoun River they get a big village there too. And that's where lots of us go up today.

"They get nothing but fresh food those days. Ninety-seven years ago, even then from the time I was born there. They fish for trout and other things. That was a rich river that time. Lots of geese and ducks. But today white people don't allow them to get it at any time, just certain time they give them... and it's short too."[59]

"When garden's finished, up to Yakoun Village. Men used to trap for bears. Trap up at the falls for spring salmon. When the spring salmon go up they jump up on the trap. Smoke the bear meat; smoke the seal meat.

"At Christmas they'd take it down to Massett. My mother used to give it to people who would like it. And they'd give her something back,

like kerchief, clothing, shawl. After Christmas go back up again. That's
when the steelhead come down. Change their skin. So red. That's when
they start smoking it."[60]

TIDE PEOPLE

Mark Bell, 1989:
"Yakoun River people were the strongest. They made up songs for every
meaning of the totem pole. They had a song to everything they did."[61]

They go to Ain River first, then they go to Yakoun River because
spring salmon goes in that one. Yakoun people—great big mens.
They used to spear the salmons. They just spear them. People
that grow up there know how to spear them.

I didn't see them but lots of other kids used to go and watch
them. They catch them at the waterfall. This great big salmon
tried to jump over. And there's a great big hole underneath the
waterfall. They lay their eggs there and they hatch it in there.
And after, they go way up waterfall, way up in the lake there, and
they die there. They go up there to die. Great big spring salmon.

The spear, it was real sharp. I seen it many times. We used
to think it was so big. We always go and see when they get it. You
know how kids are, suspicious [curious] about everything. A long
string tied on a great big pole so it wouldn't wiggle away. When
we were kids we can't even lift them up, maybe sixteen feet or
more. Great big men, nothing but giants up there.

Charliegung [Charlie Thompson's father].[62] He was a great
big man—Charlie—Frank [Collison]'s grandfather. They used
to say they were all big men from the Yakoun. They moved out
when the missionary came here. That's the time everyone moved
to Massett.

Alfred Young lived there. He got one with spear. He pull it up and it's real slippery. He just got hold of it and he hold it so tight. He was so strong he make the big, big spring salmon tl'uusad [a single, high-pitched fart]. That's what they said.

All I used to hear is he used to be a real good dancer. And they used to say in olden days, real olden days, if they want them to be a real good dancer, they get a branch of tree and they rub it on the baby, the whole body, and they drive it in, put it right in the middle of the river that flowing so hard. Any river. And it going like this [arms dancing to show dancing in the river], the tree branch. They said that's what they used to do to him when he was baby.

I used to hear him singing some hymns, real nice voice. I used to hear him in record. He was blind and his daughter used to take him around all the time. Ruth Bell her name was.

Then they come from there, stay home while the winter's on. Lots of people coming home from camping.

They used to say "just like Yakoun people," when people are slow or late. "Must belongs to Yakoun people that he's so slow." And it wasn't the people. They wait for the tide to come in. They know what they're doing. The tide goes up there real slow, because way up the inlet. The river is so far out the beaches. So they were never on time. So it wasn't the people was slow, it was wait for the tide.

They had lots of patience, to live by the tide. It's that funny thing—you have to wait for the tide to come in, the tide to go out. Well, you more like tide people.

It wasn't an excuse. That's just the way. You wait for the high water. It flowing in just like a great big river. And you go with the tide, you get there real quick. If you bucking the tide you can't get there.

THE GARDENS[63]

Grace Wilson:

"I was born 1910. They used to have gardens all over. What I remember is we stay down North Island till September, and you move up and you dig your garden, and the sun still comes back, and you let it dry out in big baskets. They dug a big hole. I don't know how many sacks goes in. lining with beach board. Potatoes. They store them [circa 1913 at Shag Rock], for winter.

"Why I think of it is we were on canoe. I think of that, just like a dream to me. Mother put rug [woven from cedar], tree bark, where we sitting. Just me and my one brother, just two of us. The potatoes on the canoe and some of the grease they buried in the pit… We call it hl'aang k'aal [root cellar], where you keep the spare potatoes.

Grace Wilson of Old Massett, in 1979, gathering cedar bark for weaving. Then, as now, Haida weavers would use cedar bark and spruce root to create a basket, a garment, a mat or a traditional Haida hat. Ulli Steltzer photo, donated by Ulli Steltzer, Haida Gwaii Museum, Ph08514

"We first start garden. We used to build a [trench]. My basket was about this size. We don't carry sacks. Maybe that time no sacks. I don't know. Always pack it. My auntie's children, same age as me, my father's sister's kids. Kelps. Starfish—those orange, purple ones. You put the fertilizer in, spread it, two or three inches soil on top. Then you put the potato seeds in, two-foot mound.

"That's what they do with stink eggs. You got more juice on them. From king salmon or dog salmon. We used to get the eggs. When you get your dog salmon, wintertime, September, October, you dry your fish.

You get seal. You smoke it. Sometimes when it's fresh you cook it in a big pot. That's what my dad done."[64]

Just women, and their husbands used to help them. Everybody used to go out to the campgrounds. There's lots of gardens little ways from 7-Mile, point way out there. Jones family, like Moses Ingram's mother and them, used to have great big gardens out there.

How they get the potato here is quite interesting. There's a great big ship full of potato sacks and it get wrecked out at North Beach, all the potatoes wash ashore then. And one of the men, captain or somebody, show one of the Indian men. He says to him, "Good seed." "Good seed," he said. He dig a hole and show him how to do it. He was telling the Indian man, but he don't understand him so he says, "That white man call it sguusiid." It's good seed. So right now they call it sguusiid. That happened out at North Beach.

From that time everybody used to make big gardens, and Old Massett people, they used to take it over to Alaska, going to trade that sguusiid with some other food. The big canoes just full of other stuff. They're trading. That's way before me.

My grandmother and them had a great big potato garden across there [Yan]. There was small little houses that they used to live in there. In April everybody's across there making their garden. We used to help mother pack the kelp for fertilizer. I work like everything. You make a great big groove and fill it; the kelp's in there, put soil on it and then put the potatoes. And potatoes will be that big!

They call it dlagu [a digging stick], to dig the garden with.[65] They used to use red cedar the most. I used to know it because you could smell it. And when it's harvest time, they use the same thing, dig the potatoes out with.

Mother's the one know how to make turnips real big. They're wondering how she did it. When the leaf come out, she step on every leaf, and the leaf don't grow up and the turnips will be that big. When they leave the leaf on, it grow right up, nothing in the bottom; when you step on it, it grows in the bottom. She used to walk right on it, flatten the leaves out. It's something real tricky. They used to laugh at Mother. When it's harvest time in October, her turnips are that big. We used to eat the turnips with sugar when we were kids. You eat it as a dessert. Real good. They used to plant carrots too.

In June they go back to their garden. From North Island. They're weeding them. They don't weed them, it don't grow right at all. They have to clean the weed off all the time. Row all the way down. You start off in the morning and you get there quite late in the afternoon, row all the way down.

Anyway they used to have a good time on the way to North Island. Camp there. Have a lunch there. And then from there they started off. I think it takes all day long to get there. It seems to me it wasn't too long. One captain knows the paddle, the one that steers the boat.[66]

I saw Dad and them used to have the potatoes in the cellar. Potatoes—it grows so big, and long.[67] That's from Alaska people's side, they said. We used to take it underneath the basement. We work real hard.

I remember I used to think that Yan beach was big place. I just saw it last spring. It's just a small.

We don't allow to go out at all because there used to be lots of people live there and there's dead people on a tree [a mortuary pole] there. They used to keep on telling us not to say anything around there. There's too many ghosts around there. That's what we used to be afraid of.

They say rich people have gold bracelets right up to elbow, and they don't supposed to keep anything from dead people. They buried them with it. They said Mr. R. take all the gold bracelets from it. He take all these Indian stuff to Victoria and sell them for prices. Take all what Indians used to [be] so scared to touch. He take all those Indian stuff. Even Lepas Bay. There's a great big cave there, on the way to Lepas Bay, lots of gold; that's where they used to take it when they die.

In the olden days, they dig a great big hole, to keep all the jewelries. Kilaads [Tsimshians] or someone may go through there [and take it]. They bury them under the trees. Someone will find some someday. When I was a kid, they still think a lot of them. Later on, they just threw them away.

In April the whole village move down to Daadans [Dadens].

Nora remembered that each spring everyone would move from Massett to Dadens where salmon were plentiful. Dadens lay across the pass from Kiusta. In late summer/early fall many would move up the inlet or to Naden to fish the rivers. Mrs. G. Kelly photo, 1889, H.B. Phillips and Betty Dalzell Collections, Haida Gwaii Museum, Ph03427.

NORTH ISLAND

North Island was just like bread and butter for everybody. They used to move down there every summer. They start to move down in April. April, May, June, July. Nobody in Massett. In August everybody coming home. It was just like holiday. I used to like it, to play in the water.

There was no clam diggers those days, no cannery, so everybody used to be home, till springtime they go to North Island. Mens are trolling there, at North Island. They used to make piles of money, some men. Lots of spring salmon.

About this time everybody so happy because they're all moving over, just like if you going to Hawaiian Islands. So many fish there, and that little bird sG̱idaanaa [ancient murrelet].

We go on the rowboat when I was a kid. Everybody's fishing in a rowboat then.[68] You ought to see the rowboat, millions of them. They row and the boat was just loaded down with spring salmon, real big ones.

Even womens used to go out, row on a boat and fishing. I remember Augustus's mother used to fish out there. Fanny Wilson. All by herself too.

They used to go out alone, those ladies. I saw them when I go out with Dad. Ladies were catch more fish than the mens, real big spring salmon. Out at North Island. And they go up to Yakoun River, with a net. All the womens used to do that themself.

You ought to see all the boats, pulling the fish in by hand. They fishing there for packer come over from mainland, Claxton, a great big packer all loaded down with spring salmon and take it over there to mainland to the cannery.

I go there when I was kid. Everybody got the cabin. They build a cabin for themselves. There's quite a bit, maybe over three hundred anyway. Everybody got a cabin down at Dadens, great big village there. Dadens, where all the fishing crowd used to stay.* Florence Davidson, she's selling some bread, just for twenty-five cents, great big loaves, but you make lots of money at it.

I heard they used to have a great big feast† out there too. People celebrating something for their people that's gone. You know, put on a great big dinner, give things away. Like apples. That was when the fish packer used to come there. So they got a great big order of fruit, like apple boxes, orange boxes. And my dad got his store down there.

Same way as my uncle Robert Bennett had a store down there. I was quite big then. I used to look after his store all the time. Take all his stuff down on his seine boat, great big seine boat. *Cordelia*, the name of the boat was. The boat call after uncle's wife. Dad was helping them building that boat too. And I like to think about—there's orange, that big. The inside was red, real red, inside. They must have inject something in it, but it make it taste real good too. I remember.

They got their little houses there, all over the place. Dad got a great big cabin because we're a big family. Some people, lots of kids, they stay together in the cabin. And a great big bonfire in the middle. And the chimney like it's got a trap on. When the wind is blowing, one would sit down and watch where the wind is, so it don't get too smoky in the house.‡

When Mathias [Abrahams§] and them were just young kids, they got a little house there, about 1923. We play in the water. And

---

* Skidegate people had houses nearby in Henslung Cove.
† Memorial feasts are held one year after a death.
‡ Haida longhouses had a hole in the roof of the house to let the smoke out. It was covered by a wood or bark flap. The opening could be adjusted according to the direction of the wind.
§ Mathias Abrahams, Eliza Abrahams's son, Leila Abrahams's husband.

Fishing boats anchored at North Island, 1938. People fished all along Haida Gwaii's north and northwest coast, whether with rowboat, gillnetter, troller or seiner. Josephine Johanson photo, Haida Gwaii Museum, Ph02007

they had a great big ball field. And all the kids are playing ball. They used to have a great time there.

Everybody used to go picnic every Sunday too [to T'aalan Stl'ang (Lepas Bay)]. Everybody, but I was sickly so I missed out.

*

I left Massett 1927 and they still used to go fishing, camping. Everybody's fishing in a rowboat then. The time I was out there there's a packer there. The packer buy the fish and take it over to mainland, Oceanic Cannery and Sunnyside Cannery. So they had a good chance to make money then.

At K'yuust'aa one time there's a real high tide, been rough for a long, long time. They're out of food out there. You can't get out fishing. No bait. No way to get bait at all. They used to dry devil-fish. They dry them and when they go out fishing, they cut it in small pieces, give it to each other for bait.

It sounds not too long ago, when there's Hudson's Bay blankets, red, great big blankets. Womens get this and spread the big red blankets on the beach and all the halibut come ashore to the shallow places. While it's rough, halibuts in the deepest, and they saw this, sounds like it's more like the halibut see the things on the shore. They're hungry too I guess and they go to the red thing. People catching lots of halibut.

That's a real important story that I'm scared to say anything, because I feel like I give big secret away because halibut is bread and butter for everybody.

If anybody had a red thing on the boat, shark, great big, grey. They go after red things. If you use red things—*whoooaa*—on the boat. Real dangerous, bigger ones. They don't eat them. They use the skin for sandpaper.

They used to have a great big dance there. George Spence played the fiddle real good. That's Vesta Helmer's uncle. Great big man. For square dances. Oh he's a real good at it. I wasn't old enough then. The square dances all the time. They knew the songs pretty good.

Some people got a bigger place. They got real good music, guitar and I think violin too. They usually sing for the dance. They call jitterbug—*jeetabug, dancing jeetabug*. Real lively song.

When my uncle got a great big seine boat, new one, my oldest uncle [Ben] was sleeping on the boat and Mathias was about teenager—just when they like to dance.

He seen his uncle went to bed, going to sleep. And he take all his clothes off and tie it on his head and swim ashore where the dance is. You know, summertime, about 2:00 [a.m.], it's daylight.

At long last our uncle wake up. He miss Mathias on the boat. He start to howling his head off. "I lost my boy. I lost my boy. Why did I go to sleep from him?"

His uncle get on a rowboat and going around the point. Here he was singing a Crying Song. When anybody die, they got a song. When they cry, they're singing. He called him with his Haida name.

Here Ben Bennett was coming, and crying away, "Mourning song, mourning song." And everybody go out to meet him. Everybody's standing there. Mathias was standing there. Elijah Jones, he was standing there. He said, "I lost my boy. It's my fault. I went to sleep. He must have fallen overboard and drowned."

Here he was dancing. And uncle thought he got drowned.

SG̱IDAANAA

When we're all kids we used to sing:

> sG̱idaanaa gwaay
> sG̱idaanaa gwaay
> *murrelet when you're getting onto something*
>
> hlaa dii gaa gyuusta
> hlaa dii gaa gyuusta
> *come listen to me*
>
> sG̱idaanaa gwaay
> sG̱idaanaa gwaay[69]

SG̱idaanaa, that's a seabird. Used to be lots at North Island. It's real good eating. It was small little bird, the seabird with a white strip on the sides. I seen it. The breast meat is real thick on it.

There's a hole underneath the tree. They dig way inside. Eliza used to be real good at picking them out. You put your hand in the hole. The bird's there. You pull it out; wring the head. They had a rope and tied them on, they had just hip full, around it. When they come home their waist is just full of sGidaanaa. They think of it like turkey. That's North Island story.

One time when I live across there, Dorothy Edenshaw, Douglas's wife, she comes over. She said, "Nora, will you help me?"

She said Edward Swanson brought all the sGidaanaa, tied up together, all the sGidaanaa's necks was hanging off, just solid. Not cleaned, the feathers not plucked off at all.

She said, "Nora will you give me an idea how to get rid of the sGidaanaa?"

I said, "I don't know."

"Can I bring it here before Douglas come home? Douglas is on the boat."

I said, "All right."

We lug it to my place. When they go, we lug it back. We're doing that for a long time till it get stink. Nobody to eat it— [there's] too much. Now they can freeze it I guess. Not then. We lug it back and forth.

Not even funny, when we're scared of Douglas and the one that get it for her is working with Dorothy's husband. They buy fish at North Island on great big *Edenshaw*, the boat. And my husband was home. We didn't want him to see it. Somebody will squawk on us.

But there's another grey one, different ones, on the other side. I didn't taste it. Tasted real good they said. It was just like a pigeon. The body was so small but you clean them. Tasted real sweet they said. Hajaa [Cassin's auklet].

When they're down at Lepas Bay,
there's an island there all the grey ones.
Clean it, and great big pot.
One of the teenager girl, "Ya, I don't want to.
"Why they eat that thing?"

They don't supposed to say that,
because you can't stop eating it.

Once you take one spoon you keep on.
They have to eat it, just like if they're punished.

She keep on eating it, eating it, till the big pot was
    finished.

They said this girl couldn't stop eating.
She didn't care if they laugh at her.
She just said one word wrong.

So they used to tell us not to say a word like that.

You know what poisoned them [the hajaa]? Stale oil, from
Vancouver. White people get rid of old oil down there. They dump
it over at North Island. The ducks got grease on the feathers, so
they all washed shore. They're all killed there now, no bird to eat,
no ducks to eat. There's no seabirds left because they dumped the
stale oil in Lepas Bay.

I was down there three times with the boys I guess. Just to
get away from Masset. I take a walk after dinner and I saw there's
water running down with oil. I thought I found a oil. I walk back
right away and told Huckleberry [Thom Henley]. "Yah," he says,
"stale oil. A great big boat comes in and they pump it off way up

in there, but it comes down in the bay. Kills all the birds."[70] This is real true story.

DETECTIVE CRABS

You know those small black crabs? I was going to tell you about that. If you lost something, no way of find it. You get four dozen little black crabs, gather all these black crabs that runs around underneath rocks. You gather up four or eight dozen. You hang it up, the corner of the longhouse, on the back, about four days, and if you lost something, you talk to the crab. "Find this for me. Find it." You get all the men, the neighbours. You invite everybody for smoke. You invite them all around the fire.

There's a man lost a hunting knife and they poured the crab on the floor, whole pile of them, and everybody watching it real hard and wherever they think who got it, one of the crab start to walk toward. If you swipe it, it walks to you until you give up and give it back.

But this quite nice man, or Chief, he's sitting there. Here this pile of crabs are piling on each other. One of them start toward that big man. He start to swear at it. It walk right towards him, and he got a big stick and...

Everybody knows that *he* did it. That's what they thought. You know what? Here he's swearing, 'laanuu [cursing], and after he smashed the crab they find the knife right up in the corner. It was right in the post in the house. Here it wasn't him. That man himself put it there and that nice man was right in front of that post. That happened in North Island they said.

Just lately we used to call it Detective Crabs. I was the one think of that name. I think it's all true. In olden days nobody swipe anything. Never. They're scared of detective crabs. You can't hide things away. The little crabs go after you. My grandfather and them used to laugh at it all the time.

AROUND JUNE

Claude Davidson, on fishing at the Yakoun River:
"It used to be whenever wiid [Swainson's thrush], came.* And then they fished till the [eagle] down, like down feathers, start blowing around. Then they'd go to the Ain [around September]. They kept their time by those things. They only did what Mother Nature told them."

They go to North Island first. Making money. Trolling. For spring salmon. From there they used to go up the inlet to dry [fish]. Soon's they get enough [river] fish to put up for winter, then they go to North Island. They all go out on a rowboat. It was nothing when you get to know how to row.

Around June everybody used to go up to Yakoun River, that's what I remember. The salmon used to start going up in June, sockeye and spring salmon. Mother and them went up there. I go up, not on canoe there, just rowboat. I wasn't fishing. I was little. I used to just look after my brothers, so I don't know how to slice fish. Mother don't let me touch it. Little bit too stingy with the fish I guess. She didn't want me to waste it.

They're staying in their cabin. And Dad put a little box way up above the door, to keep butter, two pounds of butter.

Mother hear noise outside, early in the morning. So she said, "Something's outside." So she went out and here the bear was walking on hind paws with a pound of butter in each paw.

---

* Wiid come to the Islands at the end of May and are gone by early September.

Mother scream out and said, "Give me my butter!" Just as if the bear understood English. Instead of Haida, she went and say it in English. The bear turns around and look at her and he threw that butter back. Mother thought it was so cute. She got her butter back. They used to laugh at it all the time.

Sockeye used to run up there. That's the best river, sockeye. Real nice fish up there. People used to get them. When I was young, they got the net for them. That was net time. I think great big men used to use with spear. Soon as net down they got lots of sockeye salmon in there, real pretty salmon, shiny, that big. Real pretty, shiny. I used to like to get it out from the net with Mother. And then Mother and them smoke them. Big, big fish, all gathered up. They pile it on the boats. The big boat is just full with it. That's for winter. Dried sockeye, or maybe dried spring salmon.

I don't know how they get that spring salmon though. I don't supposed to be up there. I used to be sickly. My mother have to be real careful of me. Once a great while I just run up there and see to it. I want to see it so bad. Right where the Golden Spruce are.

There's a spruce up there. They call it the Old Tree, Old Spruce Tree. Ḵiid.[71] It's still up there yet. The spruce, they don't touch it at all. They have to be real careful with it. Just one tree. And there's a great big canoe being built there. It wasn't finished yet. We used to go up there and look at it.

I don't see dried halibut so much, just the salmon. I always think halibut is so stink. But the salmon tasted real good. Sockeye is the best one. And then chum. There's some at Aawan (Awun) River and Ain River, but they got biggest one at Yakoun River. The best, spring salmon. Real big. Real tender too.

When you going to eat it you toast it on the open fire. It tasted real good. And you know the ts'alj [dried salmon]—it's real nice and soft. And they keep it so clean. And then you eat it with grease. They get it from mainland. There's no oolichans around here. They trade some stuff. Boatloads of grease, they brought it over. So everything was supply for winter.

They got more than enough, a supply of dried fish for winter. They used to keep in a great big, real tight box, they call it tuut'. Airtight. Big. With the top, red cedar. And a great big dried fish goes in there.

I remember they put those skunk cabbage leaves. They dry them first. They get kind of a brownish colour when they get dry, just like paper, and between every layer of one fish there, they put that down. That's what I saw my granny and them used to do. It was that big, two feet square and about that deep—thirty inches high. And the cover, they make a groove in it. It settle right down, so bugs don't get in it.

So when they get home they put in the one place, a big long pantry. And all that dry fish, they have it quite a bit high. I used to see the tuut'. They got piles of it, right to the ceiling, great big things like that, pile up on each other. I saw my grandmother and them have these pile up, right to the ceiling. All filled up with good stuff. For winter. Sometimes only rich people they have it they said. Rich people had the tuut', piles of them, because they put on a great big dinner, wintertime.

And on the outside, painted, killer whale. The tuut', the airtight ones, had all these paint on, just like these days, with all the four sides, all red and black. The red paint, they got it from rocks, down on the beach. They grind it up. And the black ones is the same too. That's what my dad, they painted with; it lasted lifetime. They talk about it.

And then they go and pick berries. High bush cranberries. The wild cranberries is just thick, real thick, and it's quite big. They put it in these great big boxes. And boiling water, they pour it in. It's all done, and they cover it up with skunk cabbage leaves, all covered up real nice, and put the lid on. That's all ready for winter. You just dip them out with a great big spoon, in a big dish, put it on the dinner. And that's their dessert, real good dessert.

There used to be lots of wild crabapples. They do the same thing with the crabapples, wild ones.

I remember we went picking with my dad and mother and them, every basket they had was plumb full, all for winter then. Everybody used to make those real strong baskets. Out of spruce roots from North Beach. They got different names. But some of them, they said they used to cook in them in olden days, so tight. Fine, fine spruce root. You put rock in the bottom and then put the red hot rocks, that big; get the rock red hot, then put in there, cook the things in that. That's what they used to do, they said. But not my dad's time. That's past, in the olden days. It wasn't in my time, these things.

They used to gather up all the berries all the time. They used to dry them. That's what they said, but I didn't see when they dried them. And when they dry them, then they put them in the tuut'. They put skunk cabbage leaves between the berries. The fruit dry up between everything. All stored away for winter. When they going to eat it, they soak them overnight. So they mix it up with some other, just like a fruit salad.

They used to tell stories in the house all the time. My dad especially, telling stories. All kinds of stories. More like story-teller. And I get to know everything. You almost see just how it is, because they said over and over and over. My dad used to tell the kids how to catch fish, how to drive it, how to cut them out, how to dry them and prepare them real nice and clean so it don't take too long to get them dry. Dried fish is all bundled up so nicely.

He used to tell them what to do and how to do it. Some of the boys don't even listen, but I have to listen because I was the only girl. I was the only girl to wash the dishes.

My dad make a great big lunch box. What my parents used to have, and my grandmother and them. We used to call kitchen box. And there's a cover on. And there's a leg on the outside. You just put it down, and with two legs on. Taaw gudee. Taaw means food. Gudee is the box. Taaw gudee. The taaw, that's food box. That's what we grow up on. Great big lunch box, about two feet long, one foot high, with all the dishes in, and the spoons and stuff like that. Made out of a board of red cedar, one piece like. [A bentwood box.] They just built for the boat. You take it to the house and use it for chair too.

You can keep plates and cups in it, and just a few of bread and things like that. Sugar and salt and everything else goes in there. Dad got a little box in there for fork and spoons. And there's another one for like butcher knife.

Great big spoons. Made of cow horn. We had lots of them. And my dad make some small ones for us. You eat it out of that great big spoon, get nice and cool by the time you eat it. My dad used to make them. I used to see other people made it out of yellow cedar, the toughest kind.[72]

An iron cooking pot would be used to cook over an open fire. Dot Lewis photo

Pot was that small with four legs on. You can put it on the open fire to boil fish in it. There's an old lady. Their husbands used to go to mainland on canoe and the canoe tip over. Everybody got drowned.

Somebody said, "I wonder how they going to break the news to her?"

"Got some news to tell you." And she sit.

He said, "Oh dear. Your husband got drowned with other people."

She said, "Haajaadiiyaa," means really hard you could cry. "Oh dear. He lost my iron pot."

SO SUDDEN THEN THERE'S A SONG

Even in olden days, their parents would leave a boy or a girl with their granny. They used to say "deserted child." They leave it with their granny and his granny brought him or her up.

That's up, way up the Yakoun River. They used to live around there, to dry some salmon. They used to get spring salmon and humps and sockeye going up there. That's why they all living around there. That's a real long time ago.

They had village there. Not down at the point. Way up the river. Quite ways up, they said. My dad was around there, cooking for some gold miners, when I was young. They used to see these things around there I guess, where they used to live, but it's too long ago. It's all grown over. The trees are all real big trees now, so you can't even see it. See there's great big red cedar trees around there, great big ones.

Maureen: A mile upriver where they used to get logs for canoes?

Nora: Yes.

Way up the Yakoun River,
they used to live around there, to dry some salmon.
That's a real long time ago.
They had village there.

Everybody's away, get food in summertime
and he just a teenager boy
was left with his granny alone.

They had nothing to eat.
So he want to do something.
So he ask his granny:
"How did my uncles used to trap for bear?"

So his granny show him how to trap for the bear.
"Get the little branches, whole bunch of them."
So she make a big hole like supposed to be,
but in the house.
She show him how to make the trap for bear,
great big bear.
It has to be great big logs
but with a twig she give him the idea how the trap.

So he got little sticks and his granny show him.
Dig a hole there and the trap's standing there.
The bear tree used to be real thick,
real big and real hard they said.
Used to be great big trails,
the bear trails,
and she told him to build this up and she show him
        how.

There's a bait hanging there.
The bear going to get it.
They used to make rope out of cedar bark.
Real tough they said.
It's hanging there.
So the bear walks in there and get the bait
and then the trap goes right down on.
The whole big thing comes down and kill the bear.

After he's through with it,
he went up to get some big logs
and put it up there himself
on where he digs a hole.
He got some logs.
He's big enough to cut that log.
And then the trap underneath.
Big hole there with a trap.

They used to check on the trap, about two days' time.
When he got there, the trap was down,
so he know that there's a bear there.
He went up there,
sure enough, the bear was killed.
That big log hit on the head and died there.
So he tried to get the logs off.
He take everything off the bear and he tried to pull it.
He couldn't budge it.
It was so big he couldn't handle it.

It was too big.
He was just a little boy,
just like your boys I guess.
Too big to handle.

He walked; he tried,
and then it didn't even budge.
Too big.

He walk around.
He didn't know what to do.
Too big to handle,
too heavy anyway, great big huge thing.
So he walks around the dead bear two or three times.
He didn't know what to do.
And then, so sudden
there's a song goes in his mind.

"What kind of big animal you are?
I'm little bit too young for you,
to handle you."

That's the way the song is. SGaanaas means great big animal.

Guustaa sGaanaas 'ii jaa duu
*What big kind of animal, the way you're laying down, the
way you laid?*

guus sGaanaas 'ii-jaa-duu
I wonder what kind of supernatural being you are

tll-guu daa-aang kuu-uu-daang
that you are lying there that way

daang-kaa dii kaa-hii-daa
for you I'm too weak

daang-Gaa dii kaa-hii-daa
I'm little bit too young for you.[73]

That's what the last verse.

And when he tried,
it was just like a feather.
He went there
and he handled real, just real light,
after he sung for the bear.

So he take it home
and his granny—
they used to smoke them in olden days.
They got lots of things to eat.
They got so much to eat.
He skinned the bear and make a coat out of it
or an apron.

So anybody can do that.
If they listen to their granny;
make a long life and real wisdom.

That's at Yakoun,
way up at Yakoun River.

When he grow up he make all kinds of fur things to
    wear,
apron made out of martin skin.
Make real expensive-looking things.
He got lots of martins and make a coat for himself.

His first cousin,
a little girl,
used to sneak out to meet to him,
when they were real poor.
After he finish his cape,
he's taking a walk in the town,
and the girls would peep at him.

And the girl same age as him,
the girl that he's supposed to go around with I guess,
"It was just little while ago
I used to see you hanging down."

I can't explain it in English.
She means: "You used to have no clothes on.
I used to see your privates. Now you're a big shot."

So this girl said, "I just seen you not too long ago.
I seen everything what you got."

And this man turns around and he said:
"That's what we growing up for,
to get different,
get real high.
We grow up for big change, get rich.
That's what I grow to be."

That song goes with that story. There's so many verses to that song. Everywhere my dad act, he put the words in.

And it sounds like Skidegate people, the way they talk. We don't talk like that, but in that song it sounds like. We say sG̱aanaa, for big animal. Skidegate people say SG̱aanaas.[74]

And here sure enough, Mr. Young from Skidegate is the one that teaching my dad that song, about ten verses on. I just know just one verse, and the chorus, most of it. I was sorry that there was no tape then, those days. It will be worthwhile. Of course they didn't know it's going to come in handy.

Lots of young kids want me to teach them this Bear Song. I had lots of rides for that small little song that I learned from my dad.

One time there's a concert, and I told them somebody has to be bear, and I was the bear.

If you learn one song or two, you can pass with it. When I grow up, I found out everybody ask me to play this and play. That's a million dollar song. Many times I get paid real good from the audience. And then, it's worthwhile to know Haida songs these days. I was sorry I didn't learn more. I just know about three. That carries me all over the place. Travel with it too. If only I know more than that, maybe I keep on taking long trips.

It wasn't the grandmother singing, it was himself, just a teenager boy. That's different altogether when they act it. I don't like that. That was him that start to sing. That song got in his mind, not his grandmother.[75]

They used to tell us not to make fun of anybody like that

Naanii Nora on a moss seat at the T'aalan Stl'ang Rediscovery Camp.
Thom Henley photo

Returning home from fishing, Massett, 1911. Schooners are harboured in the tidal slough in the background. Mrs. Van Frank photo, H.B. Phillips and Betty Dalzell Collections, Haida Gwaii Museum, Ph03114

because they grow up, and a rich man. They used to get real rich. They'd drink some kind of medicine to get real rich. They drink medicine so much that they got rich.

It got in my mind. Why they get so rich? You know why they got so rich? They were healthy. Your whole body is healthy. If something wrong with your stomach, you can't work. When you're healthy, you do everything.

AFTER EVERYTHING'S OVER

Claude Jones:
"Ain—every family had a great big smoke house, forty foot long, smoke and dry dog salmon in the fall time, then started to jar fish. They only jarred white springs at North Island."

After everything's over, around September they all go up the inlet, Ain River and Awun River and Yakoun River. That's where they put their fish up for winter. Some people go to Naden.

Dog salmon and coho, chum they call it. And the humps [pink salmon] are all gone then. They got a great big hump on—it good for nothing. That's why they call it humps. September-October, that's the end of it.

The humps used to be so thick. Real lots. You can walk on it, that's what they used to say. You can threw paper on it—it carries the paper. That's what Mr. Robertson used to say. You threw paper on the humps and it carried on, floating on them. That's how thick. Just like that. I've seen it many times.

The humps goes up the inlet, up to the river. A few weeks after that they all go died. They go up the—they call it waterfall. There's a waterfall like that and the humps jumped up, everyone. They go up to the lake in the middles, that's what they used to say. Some of them couldn't make it, some, where they went up the lake. So somehow they all died there. That's the where they go to die. And they got the eggs. Lots of small ones then.

You can't sell them from the river. They don't sell any kind of fish from the rivers at all. Real strictly against the law. Even those days there was the fish commissions watching them. Eddy Singer and Wes Singer is the Fishery mans.

They start to even don't let people halibut fishing little ways. They stop that. But Willie Matthews, that's Phyllis's dad, went out there just on purpose. So they tow him in for biggest trouble and they stop it. It's going on yet. Indians can go out and get their own fish. Willie Matthews started that. He do that on purpose. They must have a meeting about that. He go out there right where against law. The Fishery, big boat tow him in. From there they pass that Indians can go out and fish for themself. That's a real smart idea. If he didn't do that it will be strictly law yet, for Indians.[76]

Charlie Bellis:

"There was a Native Brotherhood meeting about fishing rights. Trial... a trial in the Village Hall, for fishing halibut outside the boundary. They were fishing out here off Straie Island and it was inside the halibut boundary. So they got pinched.*

"So it was a great court case and a lot of letter writing between the Indian agent and Fisheries. Big trial—1935. Bob Mallory's father was judge, from Port.

"The regulations said 'no person or persons.' The verdict was that the regulations made no reference to Indians. Not guilty.

"They decided that Indian people are not people. Willie Matthews used to tell me the story and told it to me and told it to me... International Halibut Commission—it was not their intention to deprive Indians of food fishing.

"Some thought at the time to closing sea areas for Native food fishing, i.e., from Sandspit to Lawn Hill for Skidegates. Father Las Cascas made this argument 500 years ago—taking land from North and South America was wrong.

"The Sparrow Case said that Native fishing rights are a communal right, not individual. I can launch a class action against Mac & Blo."[77]

Everybody used to be up there, drying fish at Ain River. Just like a great big city there. It used to be real good. Everybody got a cabin and then this big smokehouse together. Somebody use this part; somebody else use this part, all in corners. It used to be real good.

I remember just once a great while, people run out of food. Ladies, they start to picking spruce cones. They top the trees. Their boat was just loaded down with cones. In a big sack. I think they're five dollars each. I remember everybody making quite a bit of money.

---

* Willie Matthews, Jimmy Harris and John Geddes had deliberately challenged the regulation. They were charged.

Dad goes out trapping and we used to go with him, just for fun. I was the only girl amongst the boys. I used to go with my dad, just to get out, up in the bushes, two or three of my brothers with us, and another boy. Just to hiking around. I rather go around with them than stay home and do nothing. They don't stay there too long. They usually come home right away. Settle down for winter. Everybody.

My dad got us those high boots. I remember at Ain River. I got four brothers. They all had high boots. When we come up, it lay right by the door, pile of them. When it's cold, they got a tent inside the cabin. That's what I used to sleep in, a tent inside, so you don't even feel it's cold.

And at Ain River there's a great big tobacco garden. A rich man has to have it, and he hire nothing but a pure girls [virgins]. And they usually have a great big smoking party, just like a great big dinner. They invite a whole bunch of people. The water was all around there, but my mother used to tell us—that's the where they used to grow tobacco [Haida tobacco]. They dry them. And when they dry them they keep them in a tuut' laa [nice food box], a box, with a picture on it.

[Late fall] some people go out trapping, for land otter. It's so hard to get though. That's the way they make their money.

IN MY TIME THEY COME HOME

All I can remember, the men all get wood. I used to see them cutting wood all the time. The time is not like these days, electric or oil, just wood.

The mens have a meeting about things all the time. When we were kids, they never invite womens. I was going to tell them, "Why womens don't go to mens' important meetings?"

It's a feast. I remember mother and them always invite mens along. Maybe women eats too much. I remember my dad used to bring whole pile of food, in a big bag. Ḵawk'ahl.[78] And we used to wait, wait, stay up till Dad comes home from the feast.

I remember the time they start talk about the land. They used to have a great big meeting. Some white people come. That's the Land Question they call it. Some kind of really important talk about the land.

Women usually do home work anyway. They used to weave, weaving baskets all the time. They make piles of them too. They go away and sell them to mainland. The ones that they can pick berries in and the one that they can—

Red cedar bark. They go way up in the bushes, quite far up too. They use the great big cedar tree and they got an axe and cut it round. They make it [cut it] about eight inches, and they start to pulling it. They go way up till it [the bark] gets so small and then it drop down. As you slamming [your hands] down it coming off real good. They pack it all home just the way it is. When they get home they take the barks off. And then the inside [bark], they use it for basket. But some people leave bark on; make the basket look real pretty.

If it's sunshine they hang them [the bark strips] up on clothesline. They get dry. Every fine day, they lay it out in the sun. It gets real nice and white then. But if they let it lay around, it gets darker. And then they bundle it up, fold it up and tie it, and when you're ready to work on it, you split them again, make it thinner, to make a basket or a rug. It look real neat.

Eliza, my sister, and my mother used to make baskets. Pass the time. They hang them up. Great big baskets, square ones. They make a rug to sleep on. They say it's real warm. They gather it up to take it over. When they go away, they sell them. They used to sell them pretty good. I could easily learn but I just had no time, besides monkey around. I'm sorry I didn't take lessons. It would be real good. But I got enough to do now. Too much.

This is old, old story:

> One time at Yakoun River
> the snow was so thick
> and north wind.
> And there's a kind of a young man.
> He was all by himself, real cold,
> and when everything freezing.
>
> And he could hear somebody talking.
> "I'm nice and warm when everybody's cold.
> I'm nice and warm."
> Kind of a sassy way.
>
> So he look around.
> "What was that talking?"
>
> Here it was that red cedar bark,
> made out of those rug,
> real old one laying on the ground.
> It start to move like this and it talking.
>
> So he go and put it on himself.
> He get real nice and warm.

That's the cedar bark story. Real good one.

There's a preacher, Collison his name was, when I was a kid, that can talk Haida just like Haida. Used to preach in Haida down the village, preaching from the bible with every word in Haida. He just talk plain as can be.

Henry Edenshaw is the preacher. That's Vesta Hageman's dad. Real good preacher too. Like Elijah Jones in my days when I was kid, they were preaching. David Jones and some others. Whole bunch of them, preaching, taking turns. And Frank Collison's grandfather, Charlie Thompson, was a real good singer.

In my time they used to go to Church Army meetings all the time, every night. They having a great time all the time. When I was a kid, that's all wintertime they do. Around 1925, I used to go down there to Church Army with them. I can't stand go without party.

You know where [Molly] Yorke's place is down there? They call it K̲'aayang. That's separate from Massett then. You must remember; the place where they stay is called K̲'aayang. Around there the people from Yakoun River started Salvation Army. After the second Salvation Army was up, way up on this side.

Everybody was Anglican Church down there. You know where your place is. Around there there's people from Yakoun River started Salvation Army up there. It faded away, I guess. It's Salvation Army there.

I HAVE TO TAKE IT WHAT I GET

And then come September, October, November, they used to choir practice for Christmas. They practice every night too. When Christmas over, they start to practice for Easter. Just children used to try to celebrate in Halloween Night. But they didn't, not too much. Just the church thing was going strong. That's why we know so much church songs. The church is just plumb full, where the choir seats are. Everybody that can sing, can read, everybody's in the choir. After I grow up I started in the choir. I been in the choir since I was maybe sixteen.

Everybody make great big fuss over the Christmas. But of course everybody believe in Santa Claus then. You have to be real good to get a present from Santa Claus. When Christmas come, we used to believe in Christmas so much.

Andrew my cousin stayed with us. My dad got a great big house. We sleeping upstairs. We all move downstairs for Santa Claus to come in. Andrew Yorke, that's my dad's sister's boy, and Archie and Percy and me, four of us, come down from the upstairs where our bed is. Make a bed on the floor. Percy, Archie, Andrew and I—we all get to bed in a corner. So Santa Claus will just get us.

I was the one going to see if Santa Claus come in. I went to sleep first. And when I wake up in the morning, there's two dolls under my pillow.

My dad put all the real cheap toys—in the store for ages. He got ugliest dolls in a big box full. Nobody even look at them.

Christmas time, this ugly doll by my pillow. I was so mad at Dad.

The boys got a wooden thing. You pull string and it goes. It's been in my dad's store for ages. And Andrew Yorke was so pleased with that wooden thing. Here they were so happy. Here I was mad over my doll, ugly thing. Just made out of a straw. Just the head, white and black on top, and the arms were real ugly too.

They must have give them to them when they buy some stock. Get it free. Great big box full of it in the store. That's for everybody. Anybody comes around has to get an ugly doll.

We so disgusted. We seen those damn thing every day since I was just tiny kid. It wasn't Santa Claus at all. I never forget it because I was too disgusted. There was no Santa Claus. We don't supposed to talk back to our parents those days. I have to take it what I get.

CHAPTER 5

They used to explain to us what's the meaning of it

Years ago Nora telephoned with an urgent message. I answered the phone. "Tell G. it's just like you go against a great big wall, you don't know where you come from." Then she hung up.

FULL OF HOT AIR

Claude Jones:
"If you were related to each others, you couldn't get mad at them if they pulled a trick on you."

How do you name your child? How you name them when you love them? There's lots of pet names. Like when anybody they love it so much, they always call them Guugaas [dear]. Gunee [little boy]. Skundal [little boy]. Diinaa [Mine].

Ḵaa-ang Ḡahl 'll kya'aang [He's named after his uncle]. They call them after their uncles, whatever our tribe [clan] had. Every tribe had their own names, not other tribe. Different tribe had other names.

So with anybody, strangers come in, the ones that understand our way of do things around here, they recognize them with their Haida names. This is the where she comes from. That's what it'd say. They would say, "My name is Gaadgas" and they would say, "Oh, she's a Yahgu 'janaas."[79] That's all.

The names belongs to one tribe and young boys or girls don't understand it these days. I don't think their mother told them. I don't think so. But we recognize somebody with their Haida name. Oh she belongs to this tribe. Without anybody tell them, they understand it—what tribe *she* belongs to, or what tribe *he* belongs to.

All the ones that haven't got a name they're just like they're just drifting around. You belongs to nobody. It make anybody feel hurt. If you belongs to a tribe, you in the tribe and everybody love each other.

We had two names [crests], a Killer Whale and a Raven. That's the tribe I am. Winnie [Yeltatzie] and them are Frog. But we used Raven or Killer Whale. If I had something on they know what I am. That's why you have to use it. I would use Killer Whale crests, so they know that I belongs to Haida tribe. Killer Whale and a Raven. They're together. So I got two crests.

And the Eagle tribe—all the Eagles belongs to each other. They think the world of Eagle tribe because they fly so high. But Eagle catch some fish for himself. He flies so high he can see the fish down in the water, even though he's way up in the air. He scoop down and get the fish with his claws. He pick it up.

They said he eats the whole thing till he start to falling back. That's how filled up. So they kind of making fun. "He must be Eagle, eat so much, till he falls back." Eagle is real greedy for his stomach. Eat up a whole big fish, finish it up. If anybody's Eagle, they always said, "That's the ones that eat up a whole big fish." They don't get mad at each other over it. But the Eagle was kind of great big man. He wasn't too bad at all.

Yaahl is SG̱aank'aldaas—that means Raven is wild.

> Yaahl gingaan 'll K'uhldagangs ahluu
> He-she always steals like Raven.[80]

Raven is real wild one and he swipes things all the time. That's why they call him thief. They always say "Raven—he's a thief." They call them the Raven people, that swipe things all the time. That's what they used to say when we were kids. Raven's a thief.

Only smart people can thieve things. They get away with it.

The most tribe is Eagle. Some others are black Ravens. The tribe of Raven I don't know how it start. They always look down on Raven but Raven was really naughty. They said he lies so much. Nobody could understand him because he's real naughty, naughty, naughty, naughty. Real bad boy.

You're just like Yaahl, they say, anybody that's full of hot air. The Raven used to know everything. He's so smart. Full of BS all the time but make people *believe* it.

Me? That's what they always said, "She's a Raven. She's real naughty. You can't get her to do anything because she's too naughty."

See the Raven was real smart they say, doing things tricky way.

STL'AK̲AM

There's a story that a Butterfly and Raven were together. Stl'ak̲am we call it. That's Butterfly. They tried to be partner, but Raven try to get the best of the Butterfly all the time.

> So one day they're hiking,
> walking, walking.
> And they get hungry.
> There's a great big river.[†81]
> They have to cross the river.
> And there's a log across the river.

And the Raven says to the Butterfly,
"Now you go across. Go over the river.
Go. Walk on the road.
Walk on the road.
You walk across first and
I'll go after you."

And the Stl'aḵam said,
"No, I don't want to.
You might trip me over.
If I go you're going to throw me over."

"No, no. I wouldn't do that.
I wouldn't do that."

And he says, "No. You could go over."

And the Raven says, "No, no, you better.
I wouldn't trip you."
He coax him and coax him.
At long last he got him to.[†]
So he did.

They get hungry.
When the Butterfly's going halfway,
he flipped the log over,
roll him over and drown him.
He went and cut her guts up
and eat up all her guts.[†]
The Raven eat the Butterfly.

That's why they always say Raven's a thief. He went and kill his own friend to eat his* guts out. The Raven did that. That's only fairy story I guess. They used to laugh at it all the time. It sounds like Yakoun River, the way the river started and all that.

I could see Raven—the way the kids dance, sideways like—I saw Raven walk like that. I forget where I see it. It go like that and then it came around and go like that. Two step.

PEOPLE BLOW AWAY

And some people blow away belongs to Grace Wilson's great-great-great-uncle. They said there's some Hawaiian Island people, they look like Haida there. They give them a land there to live there but there's a whole pile of them, but they don't mix with nobody. Haida just think it was Haidas.

They blew away on a canoe, great big canoe, and they didn't come back. They're still there yet, they believe that, because whole bunch of people really look like Haida.

They said—Jean, Mary Ann and them keep telling me, there's one, the actor really look like me, and she's real funny, "Just like you momma." Where they play guitar.

JUST LIKE AN OLD TIME STORY

Potlatches were made illegal from 1884 to 1951. Song and dance were continued privately in homes, with drawn curtains. Later, when

---

* Speakers of the Haida language often used he/she and her/his interchangeably when they spoke English. The language does not distinguish gender in the third-person singular.

political meetings were outlawed, political discussion, networking and planning were carried on within the fishing fleets.

Charlie Bellis:

"Potlatch—people had to stop—dances, songs, feasts. They imposed martial law. Three couldn't gather on the street. The only place they could gather was in the church. It's basically martial law.

"Then they created the Native Brotherhood. They could gather there. The theme song for the Native Brotherhood was 'Onward Christian Soldiers.' Alfred Adams and Adam Bell were very instrumental in creating the Native Brotherhood. Andrew Brown—they used his seine boat to go to Metlakatla.

"A few years ago there was a meeting with the elders on Stevenson Island. One of the elders stood up and said, 'Where's the people like Andrew Brown, marching into town singing 'Onward Christian Soldiers' to bring the Native Brotherhood to the village?'"[82]

Potlatch? Not my time, never. Long time past. That's way before my time. They talk about it though. It's the preachers stop them because they think they are praying to the totem. They used to spend so much money when they raise it in the old days. They give out things. 'Waahlaal [a new longhouse or totem pole-raising potlatch]. Poor people can't afford to potlatch in the old days.[83]

I was going to ask Claude Davidson if he know the meaning of when they were dancing [the Chief's welcome dance]. There's great big straw, I guess.* They put the feather in. When they dancing, the feather, the down of it, when you go like this, it stick to everybody in there, in the hall. The meaning of that is— everybody got a present.

---

* The straw is the sea lion whiskers that stand up from the headdress and hold the eagle down. They dance and shake their heads and spread the down.

Great big present too. A blankets, too. To everyone. Dishes time, hey. Everything that useful they give. They gathered up a great big house full of it, when they going to do something like that. Potlatch. So, they used to work real hard. They gathered food up. Feed everybody that comes in. And the dancer come in.

They got their Indian blankets on, but the one that acting had the big mask on. Great big mask, put blankets around. Soon as they sing, all the kids screaming they said. I only see once or twice but I remember it so well.

I laugh to myself when I think of one time there's a big dance and they call it saagaa[84] you know. My grandfather and them used to see it. My grandfather telling somebody else—I used to listen to it.

The story is, there's some actors coming. They make a great big long pole. They fix a big pole where it could break easy when they hit that. They come in.

There's a man come in, dancing away. And there's another one come in.

"Yaa laa 'laasii." Somebody was walking in, singing, and somebody supposed to hit him on the back. And this thing [pole] will break on his backbone. He would sing, "Yaa laa 'laasii" when he go down. I used to know the tune. "Yaa laa 'laasii," *Raven, Raven, good.*[85] And here this actor went and hit him where it's not made for break.

He sing [falling down], "*Yaa*
        laa
            sii 'laa."

I used to think it was so funny. They used to laugh and laugh at it. They used to have good times. I thought it was so funny when my grandfather or my dad or somebody tell it. He hardly say something what he supposed to.

The missionary thought they pray to the totem pole because they put it right on the doorway.[86] Big hole in it. Right front of the house, warehouse. It stand right in the middle of the door. The one they call Big House.[87] The door hang down. When you open it, when you let it go, it bangs away, great big sound, like a thunder, big, great big, hanging there, big hole in it. I didn't see the Big House. Great big house, they said. How did they make the hole I wonder.

I remember Jimmy Harris, that's Guujaaw's grandfather, is acting in there. They put him on a table with a great big axe or something. They cut his head off. I could see his head far away. They fix it up just like it was cut up. Real scared. I want to see it so bad. And I remember there's men standing in the way. I was squeezing underneath, between their leg, into the front. I couldn't get there.

They cut Jimmy Harris's head off.* I don't know how they do it, but the blood was running out of it. I want to see that. Trying to get to the front. I couldn't make it. I think I was about five years because I ran away from the house to see that. I used to be so naughty—real fast one. They can't catch up on me.

When the gospel missionary came, they said they told them to cut all the great big totem poles down. Down at North Island, the first time. There was one totem pole standing there at Dadens, and they told them to cut that one down. I remember it's laying down there, but I didn't see it. That's what I heard.

The big totem pole, with all the carvings meant everything, just like a story, just like an old-time story on the totem pole. That's what my grandfather and they used to tell. Whatever carves on

---

* This was a skit; they didn't really cut off Jimmy Harris's head.

Four totem poles in Massett, photographed in the 1890s. Totem poles were heraldic, mortuary, memorial or story poles, often political. Missionaries encouraged the Haida to cut down the poles. A.E. Pickford photo, Library & Cultural Resources Digital Collections, University of Calgary, CU176155

the totem pole, that's a story. Background story. Whatever your background is it's right on the totem pole, what tribe you are. If you are Eagle there's an eagle on the totem pole. If you're Raven, there's raven. They used to tell us when we were kids. They used to explain to us what's the meaning of it.

CHAPTER 6

But I was happy at home

Charles Sheldon, 1906:

"After lunch, Mr. Harrison saddled horses and we rode through the woods toward Massett, passing over a good trail, through a luxuriant forest, where the giant spruces were richly festooned with hanging green moss and adorned with beautiful ferns growing on their trunks and lower branches. The little winter wrens again appeared; the flicker passed in wavy flight among the trees; the bald eagle was flying about and ravens were very numerous. After three miles of that delightful ride we reached Massett, the Haida Indian village.

Main Street, Massett, 1913. By the early 1900s many Massett residents had built their own European-style houses. Royal Commission on Indian Affairs photo, Royal BC Museum and Archives, F-08380

"It consists of a main street bordered by low houses, and along it were many old totem-posts... with the typical Haida canoes, both large and small, pulled up on the beach."[88]

Thomas Deasy, Indian Agent, 1913, on the people of Massett:

"They have the largest number of good houses, cattle, boat, stores, public buildings and the best streets of any settlements on the islands.... To-day at Naden harbor every able-bodied man of the band is at work building a cannery, residences and a wharf, for a fishing company.... Crime of any kind is unknown."[89]

F.H. Du Vernet, Bishop of Caledonia, 1913:

"Giving Rose Spit a very wide birth, we headed for Naden Harbour, 25 miles beyond Massett, where there is a whaling station on one side of the harbour and a salmon cannery on the other. During the summer, most of the Massett Indians were on this cannery, and Church services were held by Rev. Wm. Hogan or one of his native helpers. The school teacher from Massett also followed his children, and held school here for a season."[90]

1910

Charlie Bellis, 1993:

"Everybody in the Village had rowboats. Harry Young [Norman Young's father] built rowboats. He could produce them really quickly."

Everything that I remember was from when I was eight years old. Just me big enough to help my dad. Eliza was married then. She wasn't living with us. She got married when she's sixteen she said. That's [her children] Mathias and Eli and Lilian and Gladys.

When I was little girl, 1910, everybody used to travel by rowboats. Most of people used to build their own boats. They know how to do it. In a sixteen-foot rowboat you could fit four or five people on it. More than that it seems to me. Two places to row. Four oars. One paddle, the captain, sixteen feet long, rowboats, quite wide, just like a real boat these days.

My dad used to build rowboats. I used to help my dad. I was just a little girl. I was eight years when I help my dad. He made sixteen rowboats for Naden Harbour. There's fish cannery. And they ordered for sixteen rowboat for fishing. And Dad was building them, and after the school, Dad wants me to help him. He got paid from the company.

Down in Massett, right front of where the town hall was, that's where the boathouse was. Right front of Carrie [Weir]'s place. Little ways.

I was the one help my dad after I come home from school. He told me just what to do. You start planking, and I have to be inside holding big wedge hammer, slate hammer. It's quite rusty. Dad was hitting it, driving the boards on the boat, and I'm holding the wedge hammer inside so it turns over and it hold it tight. He put the ribs on, the ribs of the boat, and then I inside the boat. Galvanized nails they use. All the time he was building the boat, I have to be inside holding the wedge hammer.

It's wonder I'm not a real good carpenter. So I still do lots of other things by myself. Nobody helps me.

Nobody else, just him doing it, so I had to help him. There's nobody around. Everybody used to be down at Naden Harbour, fishing, or crab fishing those days even I guess. I don't know what. So there was nobody around to help him I guess. Hardly any people then. Everybody's down at North Island fishing. In April, the whole village move down to Dadens.

I got some brothers but they're just too little and I was the only one can hold a big hammer. I was the only one can help.

Massett schooners resting in the tidal slough. Andrew Brown built the first Massett schooner. H.B. Phillips and Betty Dalzell Collections, Haida Gwaii Museum, Ph3103

That was my job. I always go around do things with my dad. So I was carpenter. Take him not too long.

YAANII K'UUK'WAA

They used to tell us all the time. They used to sing. "Yaanii K'uuk'waa. Yaanii K'uuk'waa." That's the big animal start to walking in, big mask:

> Halaa. Ḵaat'sii Yaanii K'uuk'waa.
> Yaanii K'uuk'waa, halaa ḵaat'sii.[91]

That's, "Come in Yaanii K'uuk'waa." It's my grandmother and my granddad, used to teach us, "Big monster, come on in. Come on in." And then the big thing come, and kids were so scared stiff.

I guess they send us to bed and if we make too much noise, somebody would start to sing. When they start to sing, they said the Yaanii K'uuk'waa start to come in. We all get to bed right away then. That's just like a lullaby song.

My grandmother and them used to say they had a great big man with a great big hair hanging down, all tangled up, all full of tree needles. They went and killed one man and cut the hair off. When there was a big flood, North Island, a thousand years ago, big tide, everything was drifting away, the hair was drifting around at North Island.

Gagiid they call it.

They used to tell us that if anybody got, like they tip over, they got shamed. And they went wild. They're real wild. And what I used to hear, the hair is so long, and they keep on running wild. They sit underneath a tree, pitch dropping off the tree on their hair, make their hair real big, all the twists and needles.

They used to talk about witchcraft flying around when I was kid. Mother and them got a great big feather mattress. And one day I ask the two boys to roll up big feather mattress.

Three of us roll it up. I got up there. I was going to jump down from there, from the bed. I was way up there. I was just going to jump. I was going to be a witchcraft, going to fly away.

You know those oil can with a long spoke, copper? The spoke was real sharp for sewing machine. The sewing machine was right there on the table. Mother do sewing there and she left the can there. It must have fall down.

I jumped down from up there. "I'm going to fly down." I jumped down and landed on that thing. That oil can go right through my foot. It stick right in.

The witchcraft got caught. The witchcraft got hurt so bad. I was howling my head off. No medicine. Mother got hold of coal oil and pour it in there. It heal it up.

In olden days, they said, kids will never listen. And those great big, tuut' laa, three foot big, that's the box they keep dry fish in, with a nice cover on. And when anybody don't listen, they used to put that on the open fire and put the kid in there to scare. That's what they said. Just to scare, so they listen.

They really do that. Put the kid in that, just pretend to put in there. Put the kid in there, put on the fire. It wouldn't start, but just to punish them. From that time, they always say, "We put you in the tuut'." That's what they told us. Maybe they didn't, but they just made it up. It sounds too true. I used to believe everything what they tell me. Eliza's the one make it sound so true.

> In the old days there's a spit.
> On the other side there's a village there.
> They say all those Indians are real mean.
> They went over and take some boys,
> grabbed them and took them home for slave.
>
> There's a little boy.
> He was out with his dad camping.
> At lunchtime, he cooked some devilfish.
> And his dad says, "Hurry up. Come and eat."
> And he wouldn't listen.
> He just played around.
> "Come on." And he got the boat ready.
>
> So sudden, there's great big mens come out.
> The dad got the boat and way he went out.
> Two start to grabbing him
> and they wouldn't let him go.
> So another comes with a knife
> and cuts boy in half.

That's what they used to say, "Listen to your parents so boy don't have to be cut in half."

HE FINDS LOTS OF WILD APPLES

My dad was surveying the river up there, even when I was maybe five years old. My dad used to cook for the surveyors. Open fire. Dad cook for the whole bunch of white people.

One time he was up there with white people, cooking for them. I've seen a picture in front of Henry Edenshaw's house, a white lady with a bone hat. The lady want to shoot something so bad. There's a bear across the river walking on the beach. She wanted to shoot the bear.

When she aimed, the bear turns right around, stands up, hands standing up just like a man and sounds like it says, "Don't. Don't." She couldn't shoot it after that. So everybody got scared. The lady said, "You guys. You hear what he said? I don't think I'll shoot him."

In Skeena River, there's a bear kidnap a young girl.
The bear take her way up the mountains.
Her brothers were hunters.
It's springtime.
They still look for their sister;
they knew she was alive.
The bear take the girl home
way up in the mountain.

The brothers saw snow that could be made.
It roll everywhere.
Once and awhile a snowball came rolling down.

The fingers are on there,
a lady's hand on the snowball.
It rolls down from way up there.
She just play with it I guess.
She must have go up and let it go
and it come to her brothers.
And they knew it was she up there.
They went there and get her.

Skeena River story. Up the river story.

A Skeena River man used to tell real stories to my dad and he never forget it, just like it written down. I used to hear my dad telling us stories when we were young. When we get old, he said the same thing and not one word was missing.

When there were white men mining for coal on the river, my dad, they hire him as a cook. He finds lots of wild apples, crabapples, real big things.

He pick and put them in two four-gallon cans—coal oil cans they're called. Skunk cabbage in it so it don't go against the tin. Hot water with it. Let it cool. Just like if it's canned.

He tied it up real tight with great big skunk cabbage. Tied the lid down so tight. They got shipwrecked, tipped over in the river when the river was so big. He lost all what he'd been picking.

Springtime, he go back to work again. Those crabapples, underwater, ice on them. It was next summer, almost a whole year since. He looked in the water. Sure enough, he saw the four-gallon cans. It was just like fresh.

INDIAN AGENT

Douglas Jones, 1911:

"Graham Island constantly receives new settlers; men are brought to it by the Surveyors or other employers, then when the work is done and all are paid off, they set off in various directions, 'cruising' the Island over, looking for free land."[92]

Thomas Deasy, Indian Agent, 1911:

"Now that... timber surveyors and others are going over the land, and they see that there is a possibility of losing what they enjoyed in the past, it is an almost daily occurrence for them to visit the Agency and to bring before us their claims."[93]

Thomas Deasy, Indian Agent, 1912:

"Under our land laws, a foreigner can take 160 acres of land, as a pre-emption. After residing on it, part of two years, and paying $1 per acre, he owns it. The Indians—original settlers on the land, and British subjects—are allotted five acres apiece. This they cannot understand."[94]

The Indian agent—Mr. Deasy his name was. They used to help people. Some people, not everybody. But the way the parents are, they never help me at all. They don't help us. Because we don't need anything.

They talk about the Indian agent get rowboat for Augustus Wilson's mother. She's widow for long time. The Indian agent buy a new rowboat for her because she goes out fishing.

Dad used to feel hurt over when others kick about white people. "Let them come. This belongs to everybody." That's what my dad's word. I heard him say that. "Let them come. We can't live on this island all alone." People were kicking about white people come in. That's my dad was the one that on the white people's side all the time. Of course they [white people] work for him anyway.

If any stranger comes around, white people, he always feed them. That's his life. So I'm the same way too. Like my dad and Willis White's grandfather, Tommy Nutcombe his name was. Tommy Nutcombe, that's Henry White's uncle. He's the one on white people's side. I heard him in a public meeting. He was on the white people: "Let them come. We can't live on this island alone." That's just the way my dad said too.

I was about ten I guess. I could hear that man say that all the time. And other people were against it. Hope we do the right thing sometimes.

I remember my dad. Mr. Gillette was the preacher, Anglican preacher. And then he was Indian agent after. And my dad ask him, "Didn't they call, when you selling things, they call it 'agent'?

"Now you're an Indian agent. Now you're going to sell all the Indians?" He always say funny things.

SCHOOL

Thomas Deasy, 1913:
"Unfortunately, there are no boarding schools within a reasonable distance of the Queen Charlotte islands. The Indians take a great deal of interest in the well-being of their children, and will not send them away from home, where they cannot learn of their health, and where they are not in touch with them. A number of the Massett Indians were educated in a school which was for many years conducted at Metlakatla. This institution was closed, for some reason....

"We are endeavouring to wean the Indians from leaving their homes, and to remain on their land and improve it. They are boatmen, and it is difficult to take them from the water, where they always made

their living, and have them take to the ways of agriculturists. Some of the old men are gardening; but the young will go where wages are high... the children return home with sickness among them, and, last year, we were compelled to close the Massett school through an epidemic of whooping cough and influenza, which carried off a number of the children.... There is the possibility of the erection of canneries in the neighbourhood of the reserves, and this will be a means to keep the school open during the summer."[95]

Thomas Deasy:

"In conclusion, I cannot too strongly urge the construction of a Boarding School, on Graham Island, for the Indian children.... The Boarding Schools now open, are so far away that the parents are not anxious to send their children. Your Obedient Servant, Indian Agent."[96]

Charlie Bellis, 1973:

"During that time of residential schools, the elimination of the culture was all part of the government policy and part of the church policy, kind of hand in glove. People should look at it now—as residential schools as part of the government plan because the provincial government didn't allow Native people to go to provincial schools till almost 1960."

Everyone went away. They sent them away to school down Coqualeetza.[97] Mother and them wouldn't let me go. They go after me so much but Mother and them wouldn't let me go. I was too precious. I was too naughty anyway. The ones that went there, they're all dead. The ones that went to Coqualeetza school, they come back with TB in their lungs. They all died. Everyone that went to there. They're not living now.[98]

And I got five brothers. They all die. With their lungs. They went to Coqualeetza school and they come back with TB. Everyone they sent away got TB. They sent a whole bunch of children. There's always something wrong with their lungs and they die right away. Things are not right for them over there.

I was the only one what didn't go and I'm still living yet. Winnie and them didn't go. All the one that didn't go still living yet. Flora Adams, she didn't go. All the kids they sent away to school, they're all dead. Not one was living.

Down the village there's a school. The school is right down where Florence Davidson's place was. Right on the way to the church, the new church. There's an old church there and the school was next to that. There's two white people teaching and then Alfred Adams and Peter Hill after that. Indian teachers. Alfred Adams is the preacher, and Peter Hill used to be preacher too.

When I was old enough, about eight years, we used to go to school. Quite old. They used to like it. I used rubber boots all the time. Everybody used to use rubber boots, going to school.

The children used to believe in Santa Claus. If they don't study they don't get nothing for Christmas. If we don't try to learn things in the school. That's what they used to tell us. Lots of smart kids. But I was so dumb all the time.

But when I go just enough to play the organ that's all I used to do. Later on I start to read music.

You know I couldn't learn quite a bit. I was slow learning I guess. The teacher take me to teach the little ones. I remember quite well. To tell the truth, I don't know why any white man teachers come in, always choose me to teach the other kids. And I don't know nothing. Since I was just a little girl. Some others know way better than me but they wouldn't take them. And they take me for teaching the class, which I don't know myself.

I got a stick. The teacher give me the stick. I go like this [Nora motions, pointing with a stick]. And you know those great big chart, the picture like the school books pictures in it. You just flip it over and another, same as the book was.

One small little girl named Connie Spence can read real good. I always let her stand right by me so she help me with the teaching and I get to know with the kids. If anybody's stupid like that, you put them to be teacher. That's the way I learn lots of things. The teacher learn lots of things.

I used to be real good in long divisions. Later on, not too long ago, it gets all out of my head.

I look after my uncle's store. Uncle Bennett. So I know all kinds of things in the store. I go to school, come back and then work in the store with my uncle. I know everybody, just like first reader book. I enjoy showing people. And I get to know who is full of tricks too. My uncle used to do that too.

Ever since I was kid I was working for my uncle. And Dad didn't like it. He bought me a piano. I won't even go home.

About ten I guess, Mother and them had milking cows. Nobody milk it but me. I had to get up early. To milk one cow takes a great big bucket. You know mother make bread in the milk since I was kid. When there's no milk in the bread I could taste it. We grow up with the cow's milk. When I was quite old, I used to sell the milk for the ones that had babies. I make my own money all the time.

He used to be my school days boyfriend. I look after my uncle's store. He pestered me so much. Leave note for me all the time. I was just a tomboy.

One time he want to run away with me to Alaska side. He got a little small boat. I don't dare to tell anybody. Nobody supposed to know. He tell me what he's going to do.

But I was happy at home, hey. I got all the instruments mother and dad get for me. I got a piano my dad got for me. I got all kinds of guitar my mother got.

They used to get water from way up behind the church in the meadow. There's a trail going up. There's a water hole about two feet across. It's round like that. They call that little water there Halibut Eyes.

I think it was spring water, real clean water. My old grandmother used to tell the boys if you pack heavy things when you're young, you'll be real good with guns. I think they just say that—to get the boys to pack water long ways. I'm real good with guns.

That's the where they used to get water. Way up in there. If that one go dry that means everything's dry. That's the only water.

The school burned down one summer when I was all alone. It burned right down. And no mens around too. And mother and them went to North Island. Going fishing. Everybody's at North Island, fishing there, fishing spring salmon to sell them.

I stayed home. And Ethel Stanley, that's Emily's sister, she stayed with me. Adam Abrahams's sister and Carrie Weir just come over from Alaska [1916]. We stayed home. Just few of us.

And you know, everybody ran out of water down there. No water. The summer was real hot. And we got no water, no boat. Some people got boat, went over to K'yaanwan River get some water. There's big river across there with coho goes in there. Salmon. That's the where people used to go across get water, but no water at all.

There's a spark, westerly wind. Roger Weir's house. Maggie Weir her name was. Their house start on fire, and the school was right across the road. And a spark flew over to the school and burn it right up. Roger Weir's house burned down and our school burned down.

I got two uncles living for quite awhile. And the one had a store was up on the hill. Robert Bennett. And that other one, older one, is Ben Bennett. That's his house on the way up on the back. The house is not too small, kind of round, the top. I was right on the house with wet blankets, my uncle's house up on the hill. Wet blankets—they put them on. That's how it didn't catch fire too. Westerly wind blowing real hard and the spark it just float right over.

I was in first reader then. I think I go to school for quite awhile. I was only in grade six or seven. I was doing all right, but time for me to quit school anyway. Grade seven, grade eight used to be real good. The high school like, you know. I didn't go to school after that again because there was no school.

CHAPTER 7

Song

Nora and I were sitting at one of the outdoor tables at Hanging by a Fibre in Queen Charlotte village. I'd wheeled her out of the hospital where she was in long-term care and down the hill for some tea and sunshine. Nora held her glass cup of amber tea up to the sunlight. The tea glowed. Nora smiled. "The tea is so pretty. It's just like a song."

Reverend F.P. Throman, 1921:

"We have completed our new church.... In February, 1919, we laid the foundation stone, and after two months' work the people of Massett had the frame-work up and the roof shingled. As they could only work

St. John the Evangelist Church, completed in 1921, replaced the old church. In this photograph, the men who were confirmed in 1928 stand in front. Mrs. Henry Geddes photo, Haida Gwaii Museum, Ph03816

Here, the women confirmed in 1928 are photographed by Mrs. Henry Geddes. Mrs. Henry Geddes photo, Haida Gwaii Museum, Ph03817

during the winter (being away fishing in the summer), the good work had to be left until the winter of 1920....

"On Sunday, February 6th, the new Church was formally opened by Venerable Archdeacon Collison, the first Missionary, and dedicated to the glory of God. It was a great day for the people of Massett. A procession was formed at the Massett Town Hall, headed by the native brass band, which proceeded to the grand new building, singing.... The Church was well filled with the whole village of Massett, and a good many white people from neighbouring settlements....

"Both men and women have worked and given both time and money to the fullest extent. Less than two hundred dollars have come from outside, while the rest of the cost, about six thousand dollars, has been contributed entirely by the natives themselves."[99]

> Seek and ye shall find
> Ask and it shall be given you
> Seek and ye shall find
> Knock and it shall
> Be open unto you

The interior of the old St. John's church, Massett, 1888. The church would fill with song during services, which were held in Haida and English. Richard Maynard, Royal BC Museum and Archives, A-04197

Gin-ang tl'aa dang Ḵiiyaa.asaang
Ḡahl diiyang isgyaan dang 'll ḵiiyaa.asaang
Sk'adgaa
Hlaa dang k'yuu Ḡasdla.saang

That's the one they used to sing when I was kid, all the time, in the Church Army, in English and then Haida. That just like if they preaching to you. I used to like it so much when we learning in Haida. Lots of fun.

The one that I always sing was made for—Willie Matthews and David Jones and Elijah Jones. That's real good one, the words. The song composer must be real smart.

Two young men were lay reader in Anglican church. There's Willie Matthews and David Jones, reading the lesson from the bible. They come out to read the golden text.

And this old man was song composer so he compose a song about it. That he was proud with them. He had nowhere to look around and show off with them. "My dear ones. It's so beautiful." That's what it says. Real good.

That's the song I'm going to sing. That's good one. It says:

> How wonderful thing that I see.
> I had nowhere to look around, be proud with.
> My boys, my dear ones,
> I had nowhere to look and show off with your boys.

That's what it says.

> *Diinaa Kaanaaw*
> *Diinaa la kuwaa*
> *Aay ee ee ii aa laa*
> *Aay ee ee ii aa laa*
>
> *Diinaa laa slii kii dii*
> *Giis gwaay king naa*
> *Nang Kuuyuu King dung*
>
> *Diinaa Kaanaaw*
> *Diinaa la kuwaa*
>
> *Aay ee ee ii aa laa*
> *Aay ee ee ii aa la.*[100]

Love songs, it has to be song composer made it. It was some love songs but I never did learn it. Just even way before I was born they carried that on all the time. My dad used to sing it all the time. That's how come it was recorded. So that's the way I learned it. There's a couple going to get married so the song composer make this song:

> *Guusduu tlagu dii guu 'laa tlaajuu*
> What I really enjoy
> *Guusduu dii guu 'laa tlaajuu*
> Mine/my to walk together [enjoying themselves]
> *Diinang Gangaa gud ahl tlaga guu'laakwa.aawgang*
> Love being together.[101]

> The thing that I like—
> How much I like our children going to go together
> And how beautiful are they,
> Our own dear ones, that going to go together.
> What is the wonderful thing that I see.

Something like that.
Another love song:

> *Aalaa ya huu aalaa*
> *Aalaa ya huu aalaa*
> *Aalaa ya huu aalaa*
> *Aalaa ya huu aalaa*

> *Huu guu dang kaadlii us?*
> Are you leaving now?
> *Halaa dang stlaay hl duu ts'an*
> I come in to shake your hand.
> *K'ahngaa dang gudangee*
> Your poor mind
> *K'ahngaa dii gudangee*
> My poor mind.

Are you going away now?
Poor your mind, that feeling hurt.
And my feelings are so poor too.[102]

It sounds real good. It's real good words in it. Love song. They used to call it love song. And it's three-four time: *one-two-three, one-two-three*. You can waltz in this one. Real good.

Heel and toe polka. They put lots of Haida words in it:

Athlaa gaa dii guu daa
She kept me company.
Athlaa gaa dii guu daa Diinaa jaadaa gun
My girl she was.
Diinaa jaadaa gun[103]

They put lots of pet names in that song. How could we say? When you have a real good company. If I was real lonesome and somebody keep me company. That's just the way it was. But I really don't know how to say it in English. [Nora drums and sings.]

We will go, we will go, we will go, we will go,
Oh yes we will go to the heavens above.
We will go, we will go, we will go, we will go,
Oh yes we will go to the heavens above.

And:

Take me back to Massett town,
Massett town,
Oh Massett town.
There's be where I long to be.

Nora playing the accordion with Melody Daniels on banjo, Judy Letendre on spoons, Wilfred Penker on conga, at the Elders' Longhouse, Kiusta. Music was integral to the Haida. Both Massett and Skidegate had village bands. Nora played piano, guitar, banjo, ukelele and accordion. Thom Henley photo

Friends are so dear to me.
Totem poles across the yard.

There on a square
I don't care
Anywhere
Take me back to Massett town.

That's a cute one.

A SONG WAS SUNG

Leslie Drew and Douglas Wilson:
"Before and after every transaction, a song was sung. Singing accompanied almost every formal act of Haida life."[104]

Reverend William H. Collison, 1878:

"[Singing] acted as a charm also in drawing many to the services who otherwise might not have attended."[105]

Bishop F.H. Du Vernet, Bishop of Caledonia, 1913:

"As is customary in almost all our Indian Missions the morning service was chiefly in the native tongue, and the evening service in English. The Organist was the chief Councillor of the village, Alfred Adams, and my interpreter was Henry Edenshaw, both fine intelligent men who speak English well—a credit to any community. A choir of men in surplices led the singing, which was very hearty, and two of them read the lessons, in the morning in Haida, and in the evening in English."[106]

Mrs. V.A. de B. Davies, circa 1935:

"The death of Henry Edenshaw brings back memories of the winter we spent on Graham Island and the Christmas Day on which we were guests of the Haida Indian chief and his wife....

"It must suffice to mention that Father Hogan was the missionary at that time at Old Massett, a great six-foot Irishman who looked as though he should have been in the Guards and whose title was one of affection and not indicative of his form of faith....

"Father Hogan had a choir of men in his church who used to march in, two and two, in their white surplices, like a troop of soldiers.... The only musical instrument was a small harmonium, but the singing of the men—all in Haida—mingling deeply with that of the women and children among the congregation was like the sound of an organ. Edenshaw read the lessons in Haida, and when Father Hogan preached he stood by and interpreted it in a strong, ringing voice. It made one feel that they were the people and we were only foreigners."[107]

CHAPTER 8

And so I left Massett right to here

Nora had a gift for "classy split-second hats" and she generously shared her crocheted hats with visitors. Mary Ann Bellis photo

It's raining and dark outside with early winter night. The telephone rings. It's Nora. "I just made some 'pahkah' house rolls for your boys. You better come over and get it." Nora wants company.

It's warm and cheerful and cluttered in Nora's house. On the floor near the stove is a pile of tin can sleeves, ends removed, holding rolled newspaper for fire-starter.

We drink tea. Nora shows me what she's been working on. A small crocheted wool bag for her egg timer. A huge red wool rose with bright green leaves crocheted onto a black and silver tunic. I leave with the hot rolls in a paper bag and with a new crocheted pink tam on my head.

FRIENDS

Winnie and I used to sleep together; Beatrice was the fighter.

Poor Winnie. She has a tough time, hey, with her eyesight. She really blind. When I first saw her so helpless, her eyes, I couldn't stop crying when I get home.

Across here, at the corner store, she had a small magnify glass, just look at the bill, money. She said: "Nora I can't even read this." She try to look through this magnify, small magnify. Gee that's sad. And she's deaf too, but her ears is not so bad like mine.

DEADS BELL

One time there's a big family, and the father of these kids. "Even there's more flu comes, my children will never die, all, because I got too many," he said.

Everybody's kids die. It was just like the bible, hey. The older ones died and then, you know what happen? Soon as he said, the whole bunch of them die, one day. Not one left. Other people got one left but she haven't got one left. So that's why they never talk about this, smallpox.

1918, there's a flu about this time.[108] All those young people die. There's a death every day. They used to ring the bell. Deads bell. *Bing*. For long time. *Bing*. The church bell.

Every once awhile we could hear the church bell ringing. There's too many young people died so they quit it, that time.

My dad used to think the world of Alice. My dad think a lot of Lee's mother. Everything was Alice. He used to love them [Alice and sister Lily] so much. She [Lily] died with the flu down in Vancouver, 1918. She was Port Simpson School.[109]

That's the time up there, 1918. Whole pile of loggers die that time. The ones sleep up in the logging camp up Juskatla. That's white people. They're sleeping on bunk, double bunk. Bottom one, the bottom bunk, didn't die. The one sleeps up above die. Every one of them.

And you know what? All Nass River Indian, not one died that year. They wonder why. They thought they eating oolichan grease. That's how not one got sick over there. Not one died.

But in Massett all the young, about twenty years old, died. Everyone. The ones that are about eighteen, twenty or twenty-one years, no older than that, they're all dead. Whole pile of them. Real, just real sad year. Too many young people died.

1920

1920, I really don't know very much because I was working in my uncle's store. You know when you're storekeeper you're just like in jailhouse. Can't get out. Have to look after the store.

*

So many store in small village. Company store belongs to everyone down there, more like Co-op store. And another store is George Jones's store. And another is Peter Hill's store. There's plenty of money for everybody. You buy lots of things for few dollars. Nowadays cost so much.

Watun cannery,[110] they go up there on the gas boat. My dad had a gas boat, quite big one.

I work up there. I bet that's the first time I ever work. Mother filling cans. I help her. We used to work on the line, when the can

Robert Bennett's store, Massett, circa the 1920s. Nora worked for her uncle in his store. Sometimes Robert would move the store goods to Dadens for a season. Dixon Entrance Maritime Museum, Jessie Bradley Collection

going by, fill them up. Salmon. That's our job then. By the hour they work, real cheap too.

Scows and scows, and so many hump there. You can't fill them with night and day.

Claude Davidson was born there. And Phyllis Bedard was born there. Same time, when Clarence's dad had store. There's a big cannery store there. I don't know why when I dream, I always dream about that big store there. I must have liked it.

My grandmother and my grandfather don't let me learn how to swim. They don't let me learning how to swim because our great-great-great-grandmother got drowned when she was swimming. So things happen like that.

But I want to learn how to swim. I want a bathing suit so bad and then a cap. Whatever I want, mother always get it. So at

The Watun River cannery, 1930. Local fishermen would supply the cannery at the Watun River with salmon. At times Nora's mother worked the line canning salmon. Sometimes Nora dreamt about the Watun store. Esther Ormbrack photo, H.B. Phillips and Betty Dalzell Collections, Haida Gwaii Museum, Ph02213

Watun River, down where the cannery was, I got a bathing suit and all the boys were swimming around.

Here I got my bathing suit on, bathing cap on. I don't know how to swim. They got a springboard out there. The springboard is real long.

Here I walked right out on the springboard, about eight feet of water. I walk out there and I jump over. Well, I sunk. I sink right to the bottom.

That was a good one. I got a new bathing suit on so I thought I could swim. I thought if I jump and start paddling I might make it. I was older, a teenager.

You know who saved my life? It's Edward Swanson pulled me out. That's Bobby Swanson's dad. Him and I were same ages, Edward and I. A real handsome man. Oh, he used to be naughty.

We go to school together and he always swing us around and all that. That's Edward. He's so naughty.

Edward Swanson went diving in for me. Mother and Adelia's mother were howling. He pulled my up by the hair.

He got drowned someplace. He got lost. They didn't know what happened to him. He's the one save me from the drown at Watun River.

TOW HILL CANNERY

Jessie Bradley:

"Those days it was either sink or swim. At the Tow Hill Cannery milk was 10 cents a quart, bread 10 cents a loaf. There was a whole string of little cabins. They gave you a BC campstove and a mattress maybe. A stick of

Tow Hill Clam Cannery, circa 1924–30, was built by Captains Eugene Simpson and Hume Babington. Families would travel the twenty miles to Tow Hill to dig clams for the cannery, and stay in the workers' cabins. Nora sometimes worked there with friends, her mother sending groceries. H.B. Phillips and Betty Dalzell Collections, Haida Gwaii Museum, Ph01403 *wood for a pillow. There was a tap at the cannery for water. It was like a village, row of white houses, store, cookhouse. Old nonny Simpson had chickens. Early in the morning, all the little tin stovepipes smoking, getting ready for the dig.*

"Between tides, some truck driver would take you out to gather beach wood to cook with. Charles Smith was engineer for the cannery. 75 cents a box, cannery work—35 cents an hour.

"If you went early in the morning digging, then worked in the cannery, and went out late digging, if you made $5 it was a red letter day.

"There was a Model T flatbed—you piled on, hanging by your toenails, boxes, hanging onto your shovel. It would turn out at Yakan Point."[111]

HAVE TO SNEAK AROUND THE CLAMS

Springtime lately, when I kind of grow up, they used to go out to Tow Hill, digging clams for the cannery. So everybody was so busy. Four days big tides, big run out, and rest of the days they having a good rest. Four days is a great big zero tide and everybody get enough to live on till next big tide. Four times in a month. So nobody was hard up for money. They make enough money to live on till next big tide.

They got a great big camping ground. They got cabins there. The cannery built them for them. Nice little cabins, just big enough for a family. There was a school out there too. They used to go to church in the school, but I wasn't live there then. I was up here [New Masset].

We used to stay out there. There's so many little houses for everybody. And Dan Helmer's sister was real pretty girl. She stayed with me. I don't know what we living on but we out there anyway. Mother used to send some groceries out to us.

I didn't know how to dig clams. I get to know. Everything, you try to make money, it takes lesson to do it. I listen to people, the ones that are real good digger. The first time I go out there, Arthur Brown, he's the man said I have to sneak around the clams. So I sneak around.

I got a coffee store at Yakan Point when I was young. Make my cake. Pack it to Yakan Point. While the tide is out I go clam digging with the rest. Soon as the tide come up I run to make coffee. I put money in the bank.

We used to be together all the time [Nora and Winnie Yeltatzie]. We were out at Tow Hill Cannery, and I want some things at home so we walk home. Whole bunch of us girls.

"Let's get all washed up in the river there." In White Creek. "Get clean up. Somebody's going to meet me a little ways from here on horseback," I said. And I was just saying that.

We all dressed up and nobody's around but I suggest to wash up because some mens are coming to get us on a horseback. And I washed up; we comb our hair, coming home from Tow Hill.

"I'm going to be all painted up. Somebody's going to meet me a little ways from here on horseback," I said. I'm just telling lies to them. I was just monkey around. I'm just telling the girls, make them laugh.

Sure enough, few minutes after that, there's three mens come around on horseback. They think I was just telling joke to them. Sure enough, these three mens come.

It was the teacher from here. Quite young man. Alexander I think his name was. He ask us if we want to go on the horseback. They ask us if we want to ride home. I said, "Sure." I never ride on horseback before.

It's so hard to get on the horses, on the beach. The boys are helping. They put me on back of the boy that's driving. I was with the man that work at the gold mine. His name was Jimmy.

The teacher lost his cheque on the beach. It was in his pocket and he dropped it out on the beach and he couldn't find it.

HARBOUR DAY AT TOW HILL

Fussy Marks told Russell Samuels about Harbour Day: "He called it Harbour Day. People from Naden Harbour and Massett and Tow Hill would walk out to Tow Hill for a football match."

Louisa Dixon:
"This is Easter time. They're playing against each others. I never speak English till 1940. School children would sing it. I don't know how to speak English but I can sing."

Louisa sings:

Nora on guitar, making music with Louise Dixon at the T'aalan Stl'ang Rediscovery Camp. Thom Henley photo

Good morning Naden Harbour bunch
Good morning Naden Harbour bunch
You surely you look fine.
Ashes to ashes and dust to dust
If the crab don't bite you on your finger

Maryanna hee Maryanna hi
gowhilly hollo hollom holloma
Andrew Yorke's team
Andrew Yorke's team
Halloa you Massett stiffs
We come and get your team out.

MY FINGERS WAS BORN WITH IT

Alfred Adams was a music teacher. And David Jones play the organ. Alfred Adams play the organ too. Everybody was down there, Anglican Church people.

And then Alfred Adams was Sunday school teacher and a preacher. They take me for Sunday school teacher when I was just teenager. And then later on Alfred Adams want somebody to play organ for the Sunday school, so he ask me if I could learn how to read music. He's the one teach me the music. In the school he said, "If any of you girls volunteer for Sunday school teacher, I'm going to give them free music lessons." That's what I did and I get quite a ways with few hymns from the music.

Without your finger knows, I think it's hard, but my fingers was born with it. When I was just a little girl, my dad got an organ. The frame is just like little piano. So I had good time. That's the way I learn all the keys. Helps me quite a bit.

As Nora said, her "fingers was born with it." Nora on piano with her dear friend David Phillips, renowned chef and master abstractor, who hosted guests from around the world at his Copper Beech House B & B. Collection of the author

Any new song take quite awhile to get the tune straightened out if you don't know the time. *One-two-three, one-two-three,* and two-four times, the march time. The time is very important.

Of course I could play piano without music anyway. He teach me the music first, but I know all the keys on the piano already. And I already play organ without music. I just learn the keys and the notes on the line. Quite interesting. When you start, all the ABC on its note anyway, the letters on the keys; that makes it real easy. I get to know. It's quite easy for me. And I been doing that till 1926. So I left Massett right to here.

CHAPTER 9

I never came back home again

Miss D.M. Outram:

"I must not close without a few words about the new population coming in.

"Masset is growing, land is being cleared, houses going up: streets are being laid out, and roads being built.... It is also the case in other parts of Graham Island. Land is being cleared and prepared for farming,

James Martin's store on Main Street, New Masset, 1910. Martin arrived to the shores of Massett with all his store gear. He set up the first store in New Masset, which included the post office, customs and oil concession. The store was a gathering place, with political debate volatile, and Martin outspoken. Mabel Nelson photo, H.B. Phillips and Betty Dalzell Collections, Haida Gwaii Museum, Ph01785 *bridges spanning rivers, trails being made; blasting is the order of the day. On the other side of Delkatla... brush is being burnt, and every day nearly now, one may see the blue smoke curling upward, and smell the delicious (to my mind) smell of burning brush. This means clearing in earnest—a homestead—perhaps a garden....*

"The people are coming in now. The weekly boat that brings our mail always brings quite a number of people for Graham Island. There are always new faces each Sunday among the congregation....

"Our new house has been put up at the end of Collison Avenue.... We can truly sympathize with the families that come in with all their worldly possessions, homeless—not knowing where to go... [a] family from England, from a large farm in Shropshire, have gone up the inlet.... Others are also taking land up there, and will soon be making homes. Others, again, take the coast and find land along there. At times a wagon and horse go that way, but more often one must make the journey on foot. Hi-Ellen, Tow Hill, Cape Fife, and along the East coast are coming to the fore."[112]

*

Nora's move from Massett to New Masset, only two miles down the road, was an epic move in terms of language and cultural understandings. She was not only "Indian" and a woman among male-dominated white European settlers, but she was going against Massett conventions.

Early on, the Canadian government had imposed registered "status" and non-registered "non-status" classifications on First Nations peoples. This was reinforced by absorption into the norms of Haida social status. According to her daughter Jean, there was strong feeling in Old Massett against Nora marrying Fred. Married to a white man, she lost, by law, her Native status and rights.

I imagine that she made a place for herself in New Masset with her spunk, her laughter and the sheer force of her personality. Nora knew who she was. She kept her place in both worlds.

Nora and her friend Vicki Bragan were talking one day about whether to go to an event in Massett village without an invitation. Vicki remembers Nora saying, "Some people say I don't belong down there because I'm with Fred. If you feel connected, you have to be there. They didn't send me an invitation but I've got a right."

Nora's daughter Jean remembers that Nora went if she felt like going. "She used to always go. Dad never ever went down to a big do in the village."

And 1925–26, I guess, somebody sent for me, from Masset, and that's Fred Bellis. I didn't know him before. He got a job for me to work in the restaurant. And I never get back home again. I still here yet. Up here [New Masset]. They hire me to work in the

Main Street, New Masset, 1930. Clarence Martin photo, H.B. Phillips and Betty Dalzell Collections, Haida Gwaii Museum, Ph07192

The Karl Kirmis and Kurt Lindner buildings, New Masset, circa 1940–45. The building to the left was the general store—it was floated from Naden Harbour to New Masset, and later moved to Watun River to be the cannery store, the store that Nora sometimes dreamt about. Kirmis's decorative garden can be seen at the right. Captain Roy Barry photo, Haida Gwaii Museum, Ph01924

restaurant, to bake pastry, like pies and cake, and dessert. Right where the Co-op store is. I think Fred got the job for me. He just want me to stay up here then.

Mrs. Anderson her name was. I didn't cook the main meal. Mrs. Anderson's job. And her husband had a sawmill going. Henry Anderson. So I never go home again. I had to live where I work. I was living right in the back of the restaurant. The people I work for living upstairs. I live right in the restaurant for two or three years.

Baking is my job. I never did bake before, but I was getting on fine. I bake about twenty-five pies a day there. I don't know where I learn baking. Just from cookbook. I never cook before. I was just a tomboy with my brothers. And I been baking since.

I was about, maybe twenty. They don't pay too much. Maybe it was twenty-five cents an hour. But I liked it, see. Good meals we had too. All the working mens used to eat there. Just mens, and I felt real good about it. But when ladies come in to eat, I feel so uncomfortable.

I got used to the mens, see, and when there's a lady come in, I sure didn't like to wait on them. I rather stay in the kitchen. But Mrs. Anderson: "Go on. Go on. Wait on the table."

I never get back home again. I still here yet. That's the way I met Fred. He's the best mechanic. He got a house built there. He never even finish it. Right across, right over here [on the shore by the fishboat floats].

That was before everybody's here. Just few people live here. Just Indians used to stay there down the village. Not up here. Not up here at all. Lately when my children are going to school, everybody's mixed then, see.

They never mix very much; they don't mix very much because there wasn't enough people here. And Old Massett, there was no car. They used to come up, do their shopping on a rowboat. Things are pretty good.

IT TAKES SEVEN YEARS TO UNDERSTAND EACH OTHER

Ruth Turney:
"Fred was a bit of a rogue with a penchant for stories, mostly highly improper. But he was a kindly, tolerant, good-natured and practical man. He even made a brass cross with his trusty welding outfit for the Port Clements church."[113]

Betty Dalzell:
"[Fred was] always greasy, always laughing. He could make things out of haywire."

Fred Bellis (*lower right*) arranged for Nora to move to New Masset to work in the town's restaurant. They were married in 1930. Dixon Entrance Maritime Museum

Frederick Robert Bellis was born in Wales. The family lived at 23 Willow Lane in Connah's Quay, close to Chester, England. He apprenticed at a machine shop before coming to Canada with his brother Charlie. Both worked on a railway out of Edmonton. A town in Alberta, Bellis, may have been named after the brothers.

Fred married a widow, Mrs. Martha Bradshaw, who had one son, Laurence. They had two children, Norman (Buster) and Lil. Martha died when Norman was ten years old. Lil moved in with the Dunaho family, who had a girl the same age. Buster stayed in Alberta with an old woman he always called Aunt Maude.

Fred went to the Islands to prospect for gold and eventually started a machine shop in New Masset. He worked on fishing boats, repairing engines, and he ran the mission boat to Port Clements every two weeks. He was also projectionist for the picture shows. He and Nora had six children together.

Fred Bellis captained the *Western Hope*, the Anglican mission boat that brought church services and educational films to remote settler families and logging and fishing camps on Masset Inlet and the northern coast. Shown here is the second *Western Hope*, built in 1922, grounded at Rose Spit in 1938, with (*left to right*) Charles Smith, Fred Bellis, Phil Burton and Reverend Abraham. H.B. Phillips and Betty Dalzell Collections, Haida Gwaii Museum, Ph01403

And Fred used to work on boats all the time. He's mechanic, so. I fed so many fishermens. I had to feed them, cook for them. Three or four men all the time for supper. I see Arnie just like his grandfather. Bring mens in for eat all the time.

Cook for my husband, more like cooking for all the fishermen. All the time. Fred fixed the engine and as long as he works for them, well I do the cooking for those damn mens. I get so tired of it. Not just plain, it always be chicken, roasted chicken all the time. I get so I can make dressing, close my eyes.

When the low water, I had to wait till the tide comes in and then they come home to eat. That was hard. I don't like that. Sometimes the tide comes up quite late, hey. So if anybody cook by the tide, I don't like it. You wait for them, tide to come in and then come home and eat supper.

When I met Fred, well, he want me to cook for him.[114] And I just cooked for him for so many years. I used to talk just like my husband. If I talk without swearing words, it sounds too plain.

But my husband was running the *Western Hope* [the mission boat]. The preacher go around and preach all over the camps. Mr. Gillette.[115] Fred's the engineer. *Western Hope* is the, well, church people used to go around up the inlet, to running a picture show, all around the inlet, to the logging camps. That was his job. And he runs *Western Hope*. And the church people start to kick about that he wasn't married, so we had to get married. It's against law for unmarried man living with woman and work for the church.

He's too in love with his children. That's how come we get married.[116] He used to be too proud to get married to an Indian girl. Well, he talks like that. He belongs to high-class people down at England, hey.

I don't think we ever get married unless he like to work on *Western Hope* so much. If he didn't get married to me they going to fire him from the boat. Everything is against him for me. Just like if I ask him to do that. I didn't say nothing. I wasn't even feel bad about, because the kids are quite happy anyway.

Grandmother used to tell us, Connie [Webb] and Maddie [Edgars] and Lydia [Jones], in olden days, you used to get married to your uncle's son. That's the rule of it. This is quite old. They don't respect you if you don't get married to your uncle's son or daughter.

I was twenty-seven years old when Fred and I were married. We just went to the preacher here. No big wedding at all. If it big wedding, maybe we left each other a long time ago. These days they spend so much and left each other next week.

He's the man was so tight with money, and all the mens used to notice that, see. What I used to do, I used to be barber. I got pair of clippers. I was the only barber here in New Masset. I was the only one cut the hair here.

I got lots of customers. Clarence Martin was going to build a little place for me to have a barbershop but he didn't get around to it. I used to charge only fifty cents those days, but everybody used to come to me. I make enough money to spend it for myself.

The fishermens used to come and get their hair cut and I start to knitting socks to sell them. Vesta Hageman show me how to knit socks. And I sold quite a bit of them to fishermen. They used to buy it for five dollars a pair, even then. While I was waiting for the tide come in, working away so I don't get too cranky.

Make my own money. Fred always make lots of money but I can't depend on him. I like to make my own. So I get on real good. And I always be careful with what I spend, see.

I got so many friends. I used to know everybody. Policeman: "Trust Nora to find out if a stranger come in." I thought I was cheeky but it wasn't. I wonder why I get to know everybody. If you want to have friends, be a barber.

And then later on I start to repair sewing machine and I got quite a bit spending money then. I even start to fix oil stove and gas iron. I don't know how I can get it. I remember the lady, Mrs. Robertson, that stay in where David stay [Copper Beech House]. She depend on me to fix her gas iron. All you need is in that generator. You take that off and pinch a hole in it and the gas start to run. But then I even repair oil stove. I don't know how I get away with it. And I used to repair the gaslight—lantern. They use it out on the clam beach, at nighttime. Whole beach was just like a great big city those days, clam digging at nighttime. When the big run out at nighttime, makes no difference. They got gas lantern out there.

I learn it from Fred and I take all the work from Fred. He was so mad at me one time. Robin Brown's mother brought her gramophone up to get it fixed. It been laying there for a long time so we started. We fix it up. When he come in, caught us working on his shop, got mad at us. We fixed it. It start to going.

I used to get sewing machine just for five dollars, and sold it for thirty-five dollars or something like that. So I was pretty good at that.

My dad used to tell us there's a Skidegate man in olden days. He carved silver. He make ring out of fifty cents piece. He make lots of rings. And when he come home from Victoria, he trade silk kerchief, real silk ones, he traded for the ring. When he go to Vancouver, he buy some more. He sell the ker-

Fred Bellis circa the 1940s. Fred was well known as an easygoing man who could fix anything—in his own time—and was a good storyteller. H.B. Phillips photo, H.B. Phillips and Betty Dalzell Collections, Haida Gwaii Museum, Ph01912

chief for a good price. He get real rich. That's Skidegate man. He used to tell Dad how to sell things.

See Dad was making totem poles for living. He got millions of them, black slate ones, argillite. He got whole pile of them. That's what we're living on. And when I was just a small kid he had a store. When I was about teenager, my uncle had a store. I work there for my uncle, so I know how to run business. I didn't know these things from nothing. I learn it from my uncle, and my dad, and my mother too.

I save up all my money, not even spend one cent for the house. Just Fred buys the food, from Port Clements. Things are cheaper at Port Clements for him, Frank Pearson's store. That's the only place he used to get the groceries, on *Western Hope*.

The only thing I felt poor was, Fred never used to cut wood, see. And there was no oil stove those days too. He managed to cut wood little bit, when the kids grow up about teenager. I don't believe we had any real nice wood in my life.

When we live across there—Fred got a little wagon for the boys. We used to go up to the woods and get some barks. They're real good to cook in. The barks of the spruce. So I get to know how to cook in it. So that wasn't too bad till I got oil stove. I got an oil stove, later on when he's gone.

It takes seven years to understand each other. I couldn't get used to Fred for ages. He's the one don't tell anybody anything. He wouldn't let me boss my own kids. He's the one supposed to do it. He's that funny.

Charlie used to be real naughty. Of course his dad spoil him rotten. He love him so much. Charlie got a big cut. He hop in. "Daddy, I got a great big cut on my foot. Could you weld them together?" Oh he was a real naughty boy. But we love him just the same. But Teddy is respectful boy since he was a little boy.

It was sixty years ago now. Charlie was just a baby.[117] Amanda Edgars used to make homebrew. So I take the old fashioned English buggy, black one, fill it up with homebrew. And Mr. Walter Middleton the policeman walking down. He said, "Is the baby on the cart?"

I said, "Mr. Walters, don't wake the baby. Oh don't do that. He's so hard to go to sleep." Here I was bouncing buggy. I'm almost scared to death. I think I was too naughty.

"Be sure and call him Walter," he said.

A FIXER

Frieda Unsworth:

Frieda grew up at Sewall in Masset Inlet; at one time, Eliza and Nora cooked for their dad and Frieda's dad at their farm at Sewall:

"Jolly, easygoing and undependable. He'd fix you anything but you never knew when. Tomorrow's as good as today. He was a good mechanic. Great at telling stories.

"Lots of people, Natives and whites, used to buy at Sewall, potatoes and vegetables. Nora was honest as the day is long. She used to buy when we come down and if she didn't have the money then, she'd always pay it next trip. Fred didn't always pay on time. Nora sometimes said, 'Fred got money today. You better go get your money.' So honest in business matters.

"She used to bake bread and sell to the fishermen. I really have respect for her. Our first trip to Rupert, for the dentist, Nora came rushing up the plank to us on the steamer, with five dollars she owed. She said it would come in handy for the trip.

"Fred made a highchair out of pipe—welded. The saying about a fixer never fixing at home? Door handles hanging."

Howard Phillips:

"Behind the house on a slight rise of land was Fred's wooden frame, single-storey machine shop…. The inside of the shop and the ten or so feet between the shop and Delkatla Street were strewn with pulleys, pumps, water tanks, gas tanks and every kind of metal object imaginable, and Fred had a place and a job for it all…

"A good machinist and mechanic, it was as an improviser that Fred excelled…. Many a time he would say, 'Ya, I know just where to pick that part up,' and sure enough on his next trip out on the Western Hope *Fred would head for Naden Harbour, Port Clements, Shannon Bay or wherever to retrieve the article in need. In Fred's skillful hands, many an old*

The Bellis family home in New Masset, with Fred's machine shop behind. Fred's daughter Jean remembered that her father loved cribbage: "He'd stop whatever he was doing, even if he was working on an engine, if someone came along to play cribbage." H.B. Phillips photo, Dixon Entrance Maritime Museum

gas tank became a cowling for a brick chimney or an old pulley became a quadrant for a boat's rudder. In fact, if it could be made, Fred could make it and as Clarence Martin would remark, 'Fred had something behind every stump.'... Fred was also the projectionist at Simpson's picture show, affectionately known locally as the 'Olde Opry House.' Always in his coveralls, with a couple of wrenches in his back pocket, he always seemed to have time to swap a 'yarn.'"[118]

FAMILY MEMORIES

Nora and Fred's six children were Jean, born in 1927, Robert (Teddy), Charles (Charlie), Mary Ann, Richard (Dick) and John Edward, born in 1940.

Nora and her adult children (*left to right*): Dick, Jean, Mary Ann, John, Ted, Nora and Charlie. Donated by Mary Ann Bellis

Charlie Bellis:

"Father always talk and talk, telling jokes all the time. He never get up before noon in his life. Hot cakes every day for lunch. 'Tell your mother to make hot cakes.' A wood cookstove with no wood. Rain water. Dad used to call in all the fishermen for lunch, for supper.

"She's been a good mother. She was always working on food. Fishermen brought in fish, clams.

"One year [when Charlie was young] we went up and fished the Yakoun, the pink humps were running. I went up with Mom. She was working to buy a set of false teeth. We were fishing in the river; then we'd row to Port to deliver it. We sunk. This one time, we went out, it was quite a full load. A westerly came up and the waves were slopping over the boat. Just as the thing was going down, there was a seine boat sitting way on the boundary, with a set out, and we were able to get aboard.

"Mother doesn't like girls. Not hard on them, she just doesn't."

Jean Schubert:

"I was born in the hospital [now the Dixon Entrance Maritime Museum]. Mary Ann was born at home. Eliza was the midwife. I started school when I was seven years old, 1934.

"Our house was a shack, with a bathroom at the back. The kitchen was part of the living room, two bedrooms to one side, no doors at all, an outhouse, a rain barrel. We carried water from Douglas Edenshaw's house. Dad would buy in bulk. Mom would give it all away. My job was to go to the store every day and buy what we needed for the day. If she needed a spool of thread, she'd have to ask for it. Nora cleaned the preacher's place to pay for Mary Ann's piano lessons.

"No one had money at that time. For payment, Dad would often say, 'Just bring us a fish.' If a kid's bike needed fixing, he did it. After supper we'd have the gas lamp on and we'd play Monopoly. There were so many of us and we always had an extra man at the table. I resented that.

"He loved cribbage. He'd stop whatever he was doing, even if he was working on an engine, if someone came along to play cribbage.

"I visited the Ruttons, Dutch Annie. I would go over there a lot. Big house, with a windmill. I used to go over there and play. She sang, 'Oh my darling, Nelly Gray. They have taken you away.' It made me cry when I heard it later.

"Old Mrs. Martin made homebrew and got mom to sell it for her. But Rita [Pongs, née Martin] put a stop to that.

"I left when I was fourteen, nearly fifteen, in grade nine. I stayed in Prince Rupert at the Ridley House, run by the Anglican Church. There were three houses. Board was twenty dollars a month. I was the oldest. I had to work really hard. I had to get up earlier to make breakfast; then there were morning prayers. I was homesick, but I wasn't mad at Mom. I wanted to go to school. When Dad came to Rupert, he took me to the Capitol Theatre."

Mary Ann Bellis:

"Gertie Shannon, Andrew Brown's sister, lived in Prince Rupert, on the pipeline. To get to her place, you had to cross a little stream. She always sang, 'I'm a long way from Tipperary' when she drank. I always thought she came from Tipperary. I used to wonder about Tipperary, what it was like.

"I remember [Nora] left a couple of times. Once, gone all summer picking apples in the US, Dick and John and I, we set up a wooden box on the hill and we sold everything. Dad wouldn't let them sell her clothes, as if he hoped she'd be back. We fought about it [Nora's poor housekeeping] all my life.

"Dad didn't want Indians in the house. He told her to kick her parents out. He was good to us kids. He spoiled us rotten. She wasn't allowed to even spank us. We used to stay up to hear the late news on the radio."

Charlie Bellis:

"We grew up in a racist town. We breezed right through it. It came out once in a while, not often though. Most people are good people.

"You are quite sheltered when you grow up in a small town. [Kurt] Lindner—he used to extend credit to all the people in Haida. And he says now that he never lost a nickel. All the people paid him. In those days people were much different. I remember when he pulled his store up Main Street. He had a white horse called Molly. Had a big windlass in the middle and the horse walked around and run the winch.

"Not many boys in town—Norman Burton, Ralph Lindner, Wainwright, two Singer boys, Squeak [Gordon] Faire, Hagemans, Grahams. The Protestant minister—Green, Doug Edenshaw. The town wasn't very big."

Jean Schubert:

"I remember, I was ten years old. I was at the Edenshaw girls' place in New Masset. It was a nice, bright, sunny morning in the summer. Mary Bridden said, 'You're a half-breed.'

"I said, 'What's that?'

"I didn't know I was a half-breed. I just thought I was a kid. I didn't know I was something else. I thought about it all the way home. But I didn't tell Mom.

"There were shows at the Simpson's, where the hardware store is. Cartoons and newsreels began the shows. We could go to the shows free.

"It was an era of distinction between races, Indian, white, Japanese, Chinese. It wasn't so much a feeling of superiority as you just did it. The Capitol Theatre in Rupert—whites sat in the middle and Natives on the sides. The whites thought that the Natives smelled like fish and the Natives thought the whites smelled like sheep."

UNCLE CHARLIE

Norman Stewart-Burton:
"He was always dressed up when he came over here. During the war he was over there in Prince Rupert in the shipyard, a machinist."

Charlie Bellis, nephew:
"We'd have to go get Uncle Charlie every day for lunch. He stayed in a cabin [corner of McBride Street, New Masset]. They had chickens and the kids would have to cut across the yard to get to Charlie's cabin. The rooster.

Uncle Charlie, Fred's brother, came from Alberta, and lived for a while in New Masset. Charlie Smith photo, H.B. Phillips and Betty Dalzell Collections, Haida Gwaii Museum Ph01452

Be waiting for us. Get us cornered in the outhouse. He was going to fight my dad one day, because he sent us to the Catholic school. He lived here. He worked in the shop with Dad."

Mary Ann Bellis, niece:
"I adored Uncle Charlie. He was really good to us. At Christmas he'd bring turkey and everything for Christmas dinner, and presents for all of us."

Jean Schubert, niece:
"Buster and Uncle Charlie came out to Masset at the same time, when I was about eight or nine, from Alberta. No jobs I guess. Uncle Charlie worked with my dad, and Buster got a job at Clarence Martin's store."

BASKET SOCIAL

Reverend Alfred E. Price, 1917:
"The Women's Auxilliary (Native) is a real live institution. They are working at present to get money for a new church... the women in various ways have accumulated $661.61 cents... I wish you could have been at the Basket Social they had on Saturday, December 30th, for the Church Fund. Several of the women had provided baskets of food for a supper. These were put up at two dollars each, and when all were sold the owner of each basket brought a little table, spread the cloth on it and laid supper, and the purchaser of it with the owner and friends sat down to enjoy it. Some were hot, some were cold with hot tea, coffee, or cocoa. They cleared sixty-seven dollars... that evening."[119]

In olden days, they used to have a basket social for the church, gather up money. The people just bet on it. Every summer. I remember one man pay five hundred dollars for one basket. Lily [Amos]'s grandfather. Emerson, he used to call, his name was.

And that year that man make lots of money. They used to say, "See what he did? Because he spent all the money, when they gather money up for the church, he got the blessing back twice." They still talk about that.

We used to put on a concert, to get the money up for the church [circa 1940s]. And Eliza my sister, one time we come out to boxing.

Eliza: "You better come out to sing with me."

I said, "Ee, you don't know how to sing. I don't want to sing with you. So let's box then. I want everybody to laugh real hard."

Fred went and got boxing gloves for Teddy and Charlie. First thing they start to box in the house. Then both of them got mad at each other. They start to fight. So he snatch them away and going to burn them up. So I snatch it away from him. I went and sneak it away.

I was real fat then. Eliza was real fat. Both of us has a shorts on. We got a boxing gloves on. People almost died laughing. Victor Adams's mother is the one push us around [the referee].

I said, "I just got my false teeth, the upper one." I said, "Go easy with it Eliza, because I just have to get used to my teeth."

She got show off so quick and she just pang me, push me down, and then she jump on me and punching. After all, I keep telling Eliza, "Go easy, my teeth. I just have to get used to it." She get show off and punching. She's not used to big crowd when they howling away. She punched my mouth with my new teeth on. People start to howling. Oh, the hall was almost go up and down.

There's some of them on my side and some of them on her side. So when she pushed me down, I had to land on a seat there, but I missed the blankets and they pull me up with my leg, behind the curtain. Selina, all the other ladies, pulled me off.

One of us had to win. She win. Here they put her hands up. They pretty near died laughing. Douglas Edenshaw still laughing at it, just like if he just seen us. Everybody's laughing when they think of it.

THE 45–70 CLUB

Vesta Hageman was living here. She got married to Johnny Hageman. Then Mathias [Abrahams] moved up here. Johnny was just born [1940]. We used to play music. We go down to Old Massett.

While Fred was living we used to go down to the village to play for square dances. 45–70 club they call it. The ones that are forty-five years old and seventy years old used to have a club down there.

45–70. Mother used to love square dancing. Old people square dance like everything. Elijah Jones, Honeyboy's dad, is a real good square dance caller. He's real lively. The time, that's three-four times. Two-four times is two step. Three-four time is waltz time. *One-two-three, one-two-three, one-two-three.* If it's fast they wouldn't dance in it. And two step, two-four times. Nobody dance in it when it's too slow.

We used to hike all the way down there for dance. And then hike back again. With all the instrument we pack. That was nothing for me.

We sure had a good time. They hire us all the time, with Mathias, Moses [Ingram] and Solomon Russ, Timothy Edgars and me. Oscar Ingram. There's five. And Fussy [Adolphus Marks] used to play with us many times. I'd rather go around with the boys than, you know, old ladies.

Moses had a wash tub bass. Somebody else got my accordion there. We used to call it squeeze box, you know. And it makes a real good—And Mathias plays the guitar. Solomon Russ. He's a real good player on guitar. And I play the guitar. Many times I play the violin. But later on I start to play the banjo. We used to have a great time.

Accordion player Morris Marks played the squeeze box. We used to pack all the instruments down there, with Mathias and Leila and Morris Marks and Phoebe and me. Once in a while they pay us, not all the time. I rather do it for nothing anyway because we have a good time.

Morris Marks was with Phoebe Davidson. Here we walk all the way for the dance, and back after the dance is over. No cars at all. That was after my husband died I guess. Old Massett, from New Masset, three miles. We walk six miles altogether. And I was quite fat too. And Phoebe was real fat lady, tall. We used to have good time anyway.

Then we go to where the air force.[120] And they had a dance out there, with white people. We used to had a great time. I was so scared of my husband when I sneak in on him [after the dance]. He didn't get mad. He babysit all the time.

One of the air force mens was outspoken. You know how mens are. "You can't play guitar. You might do better in banjo." So my mother got me a banjo—a Turner banjo, four string on. And I just stayed with the banjo. I like the banjo best. Everybody like the banjo. So.

I used to play banjo in the Legion, with Jack Jones. So many drunk people dancing away.

I have to get my banjo fixed now too. It's all went haywire. It has to go to hospital.

Then when I got nothing to do we used to practice to play for dances. My life is quite busy. I got used to it. Here if I don't play music, I be feel so miserable I guess. I can't play my accordion anymore. It's too heavy for me. Too heavy. I can't even lift it up. I was thinking to give it to Archie Samuels. Mother raised him too. He's real good on the accordion.

TEA LEAVES

During the war I did pretty good. I start coffee shop uptown. When the air force was here I start to bake just few things for the air force boys got no other place to go. Just for the stranger boys I start coffee shop.

I rent Wesley Singer's pool room for ten dollars a month. There was a store that Mr. Lindner had, and they move it over next to Henry Geddes's place. That's where I had the coffee shop. Right by the water, down by the dock. And Mr. Martin's store was right across there. The boys would like to play the music there. They used to be Mathias and Solomon and Moses. While they were having coffee, they used to have dance.

All the air force used to come in. They used to have a dance there. And we served the coffee. I don't even know how much they paid for it. Big place, big dance place. It was a poolroom one time. The table was not there. Great big place for dancing.

I got all the old Massett people make all kinds of shells, like flower vases and some little jewelry box. I sell them for them and they give me so much for it. I bake my own things, just cake, nothing else, no pies at all. During the war, you're lucky to buy a cup of tea. So, lots of money but no food to buy. So I work real hard.

Sometimes I got about ten people come get their hair cut too. It was a barber shop there I guess, time before I let the place. There's a barber chair there so I had good chance to make money. I was the only barber here. Right in the coffee shop.

And then we bought a book for fortune-teller. Jean and I. She was just little girl. She used to help me and then she got her girlfriend to help us in the coffee shop. We got a tea reading fortune. We studied that. And all the boys used to believe it so much. They used to buy the tea instead of coffee. Things come true with it. I don't know why.

There's a ring in the fortune and you could see one leaf like that. One tea was—that's him [one of the air force boys]. They left him down the village and he walk home on the North Beach side and he got lost. At last he got home daylight.

Soon as I seen him I said, "Don't you get lost again."

He look at me real hard. "How did you know?"

"It's in the tea reading." He believed that so much.

We got ration books but they run out. The milk was rationed, the coffee was rationed, but I never was out of it. Way out in the bushes, they [the air force boys] so lonesome. And they start getting us everything that's rationed too. My husband was wondering where all those coffee come from. Big cans of it. I think they used to swipe it.

Even my husband don't give me money to buy the things I'm supposed to have. I earn it because Jean was my oldest girl. Our oldest girl going to Rupert to go to school. We have to pay for her board, but it's only thirty dollars a month. And I had to work real hard for it. I make money and pay for Jean's boarding.

Jean was working in the post office and the store too, for Clarence Martin. So Mrs. Robertson, English lady, stay there, right where David [Phillips] and them stay.[121] Mrs. Robertson got a place for her. She help me and we send Jean away to Ridley Home in Rupert.

And her dad got so mad over that because he want her to work here instead of going to school. Her dad didn't want her to go to school in Rupert. And she didn't come back. She start work in the Co-op store even when she was just a young girl, and in the office. For a good many years before she got married. That's the where she met her husband, in the fishermen's store.[122]

Her dad wouldn't send her room and board. Her dad paid only two months one time. He's so stingy with money. So Jean has to work for her spending money over there, wash dishes in the restaurant after school. Whatever I made I used to send to her. And I make quite bit money for Jean to go to school in Rupert.

I just bake Parker House rolls—I just put wieners in it. When I had my coffee shop, I make pretty good living. So I could make money for Jean's going to school. Her dad wouldn't give money. Fred used to be real stingy with money.

And then Mrs. Davidson. I got too tired so I let Mrs. Davidson use the place once in a while. So she did pretty good too. It don't need to be greedy at any time. So I'd be too tired out. Cook for my husband and bake for the coffee shop. I did pretty good. I don't know how I quit it. It was too much for me, when I get older. Too much baking is too much for me.

But people kicked about it.

1945, every sugar, butter, coffee, tea, they're all rationed. And I didn't know what to get. But somebody told me to get a paper for it, licence, so I could get the sugar, coffee, everything that rationed. I supposed to get trade board licence. They allow me coffee and milk and sugar if I got that.

And somebody went and stop it. Somebody went and go up to police station and told the policeman not to give me trade board licence. They wouldn't let me have the ration cards for the coffee shop.

THIS TERRITORY IS OURS

Thomas Deasy, 1913:

"It must be remembered that the Indian is still a 'ward' of the government, and the question that is asked, is 'the incentive for progress on their part?' We have men among the Haidas who preach and teach, business men and tradesmen, men who associate with the whites at their meetings and entertainments, but they... have no privileges enjoyed, even

by foreigners, who come to the country and are allowed to take up land and to vote. With education there should be certain privileges granted to the Indian.... We have men, who were raised in the boarding schools, and some who had only a day school education, who are as shrewd as any white. Their children are growing up with the understanding that they will take their places, as wards of the government, and only in this way will they retain their land and home associations."[123]

Charlie and I were talking about the status and non-status divisions and the hurt to Nora at being made to feel outside. Charlie said, "But the worst hurt was the 1927 judgement against land claims."

When the Reserve Commission Report was ratified in 1924, the Allied Tribes lobbied hard to be heard, as a first step toward a Privy Council hearing in England. Peter Kelly of Skidegate, chairperson for the Executive Council of the Allied Tribes, was one of three spokespersons at a special joint Senate-House committee enquiry into the petition of the Allied Indian Tribes of British Columbia, Ottawa, 1927.

TRANSCRIPT MINUTES OF PROCEEDINGS, MARCH 22, 1927, OTTAWA, SPECIAL COMMITTEE. REVEREND P.R. KELLY, SKIDEGATE, SPEAKING BEFORE THE 1927 JOINT COMMISSION[124]

(Peter Kelly)
About that time, when Reserve commissioners went around and approached the Haida Tribe of the Queen Charlotte Islands, I heard this from the lips of those who were present. Asking them to state a certain area of land to be set apart for them with which they would be satisfied.

The Chiefs who gathered in council together said this, "Why would we ask you to set lands apart for us? This territory is ours and it has been ours as far back as we can remember. Any time any other people claimed our lands we disputed their claim with force. Why are you coming here and asking us to say what area of land would satisfy us?"

(Hon. Mr. H.H. Stevens)

Question. Supposing the aboriginal title is not recognized? Suppose recognition is refused, what position do you take then?

(Peter Kelly)

Answer. Then the position that we would have to take would be this: that we are simply dependent people. Then we would have to accept from you, just as an act of grace, whatever you saw fit to give us.

Now that is putting it in plain language. The Indians have no voice in the affairs of the country. They have not a solitary way of bringing anything before the Parliament of this country, except as we have done last year by petition, and it is a mighty hard thing. If we press for that, we are called agitators, simply agitators, trouble makers, when we try to get what we consider to be our rights.

It is a mighty hard thing, and as I have said, it has taken us between forty and fifty years to get to where we are to-day. And, perhaps, if we are turned down now, if this Committee sees fit to turn down what we are pressing for, it might be another century before a new generation will rise up and begin to press this claim. If this question is not settled, in a proper way on a sound basis, it will not be settled properly.

The commission unanimously refused the proposals. Government responded by passing an amendment to the Indian Act forbidding Native peoples from raising money or hiring lawyers for land claims, effectively blocking the way to the Judicial Committee of the Privy Council. This was the end of the Allied Tribes, but it was soon followed by the Native Brotherhood of British Columbia, initiated by Alfred Adams, Massett, and continued later by Peter Kelly.[125]

CHAPTER 10

And I was left alone with the six children

Betty Dalzell:
"Fred Bellis died April 16, 1946, towing a boom of logs to the Masset mill in the Western Hope. *Fred Bellis and Jim Roughton were gassed. The boat came ashore at Watun."*

Charlie Bellis:
"Just the good people of Masset—Lindner, Martin, Sam—that got us by after Dad died."

Frieda Unsworth:
"That very trip he gave me a tow to Sewall. I rode on the open deck. Then he went past Sewall to Buckley Bay. On his way back, gassed.

"He and old Jim Roughton, American, watchman, the last watchman, at Buckley Bay. There used to be four watchmen, spelling off.

"You can't smell those fumes. There was a young fellow travelling with them. He saw them acting crazy [as the fumes began to affect them]. He rowed to the nearest place, near Watun River. By the time he got back they were dead."

Norman Stewart-Burton, January 26, 2003:
"He had a wet exhaust. A pipe went out through the side of the boat, with water pumping in to keep it cool. That's why it was called a wet exhaust. It was leaking and Fred would just slap paint on the rags and stuff the leak. He haywired it, but those days you couldn't get parts here.

Jim Roughton was on the boat. He had been a hand-logger. He was watchman at Buckley Bay.

"They were at Watun River. Pat Locker was there too. He saw that something was wrong. He had a small boat tied on and he got in the boat and went up to Masset to get help. When he got back they were dead. Fred was in the engine room and the other man was lying on deck."

Jean Schubert:
"Dad wanted to be buried under the guiding light [the lighthouse that used to be near the Old Massett cemetery]."

Leila Abrahams:
"Fred Bellis didn't talk against Indians. He worked for them. When he was dying, he asked Matt to bury him in the Old Massett cemetery so that he could see the boats come in. It took three days for the village to agree."

HE WENT UP THE INLET

When Johnny was just going on six years old, his dad got gassed on that gas boat because the exhaust pipe blew open. The poison go up to the pilot house. That's the way they got poisoned. Two men died with the gas poison. Jim Roughton and Fred Bellis.

They got gassed seven miles from here. He went up the inlet and he didn't come back. I never get used to it for a long time. I think he'll come back with the tide. The tide don't bring him back.

And I was left alone with the six children. And we've been poor all that time. We just got forty-nine dollars for the kids to live on. Things wasn't too much anyway. The price is not too much. But nowadays try to live on forty-nine. You starve to death.

New Masset School group photo, class of 1942–43. Standing (*left to right*): Mrs. Eileen (Dunn) McCoriston, Marion Anderson, May Harrison, Doris Anderson, Pearl Wylie, Astrid Peterson, Rosie Benson, Dawn Martin, Barbara Holland, Gertie Wainwright, Irene Perlstrom, Ann Stewart-Burton, Bob Wylie, Ethel Minaker, Amy Edenshaw, Phyllis Edenshaw, Lloyd Peterson, Jean Bellis, Katherine Pearson. Sitting (*left to right*): Alfie Benson, Gerald Singer, Henry Hageman, Norman Stewart-Burton, Alan Wainwright, Gordon Feyer, Kenny Singer, Ted Bellis (with pup), Charlie Bellis, Ralph Lindner, Yvonne Lindsay, Mae Lindsay. Dixon Entrance Maritime Museum

His brother and his son tried to get his money. They couldn't do it because he's married man. It come to me twelve years after his death.

And I got chance to get married but I hate to get married [away] from my children. Like Teddy, Charlie, Dick, Mary Ann, Johnny. Jean wasn't home.

I got used to saving things. I never did go to store and grub up, you know. I never used to buy food before, when Fred was living. It's Fred's job.

You know what? When he died so sudden, take me long, long time to buy stuff. I didn't know what to buy at all. I really didn't know what to buy from the store. Because I never go and get. He buy the whole lot all the time. If I say I know what to buy, it was lie. I never did. I never forgive myself. But what can I do when he get the food himself and then I just cook for him?

Mr. Lindner used to write what we got on a slip of paper. I go by that and it help me a little bit. Once I wrote down "5 Alberta Rose" [Five Roses Flour], and he didn't know what I wanted. I was so ashamed, but I laughed and said his writing was worse than mine.

CRACKING CRABS

See the cannery was here. So everybody canning clams and crabs. So all the women stay home. They make piles of money. They doing piece work all the time.

Carrie Weir's the fast one, cracking crabs. Connie Webb is real good at that. I watch Connie. There's the big claws, hey. She just grab this and squeeze it real tight and there's the pan, hey. The whole lid falls right off. How did they do it? All the meat piling up in there.

Nora in 1947. Marius Barbeau photo, Canadian Museum of HIstory, CD1996-1151-010

Mrs. Simpson goes around and take the bones off. It has to be clean up. Real lots of fun work in. I work there just a few weeks but I learned quite a bit. That's after my husband died.

Mrs. Edenshaw, Dorothy Edenshaw, they lost their big boat and she was at home. And there's nowhere money coming for her anyway. She said, "Nora I think you better try to work in the cannery. They need lots of workers."

"But we so greenhorn. We didn't know how to work on the crab."

"We could learn," she said. "At first payday if you make less than ten dollars we going to quit. I wouldn't let you work," she said. "We'll quit."

We make almost much as what the good workers did. So we stayed with it. Till [my son] Dickie told me to quit working.

Lots of fun. We were slow, but all the cannery workers so kind. Like, you know Horace Yeltatzie's wife [Beatrice], and her sister. They're real fast ones. Soon's they finish that, they come and help us. Because it's piece work, go by the pound. I did quite all right there, but I had to quit.

Group photo of the secondary students at New Masset School, 1949 (*left to right*): Mr. Norman Green, Emily Davidson, Yvonne Lindsay, Joy Leary, Jocelyn Simpson, Doris Anderson, Marion Anderson, Pearl Wylie, May Lindsay, Barbara Holland, Ann Stewart-Burton, Charlie Bellis, Alfie Benson, David Singer, Jerry Williams, unknown.
Dixon Entrance Maritime Museum

Dickie and them going to school so Dick said, "Mom, I don't want you to go to work in the cannery. We going to school is important thing. You better stay home and cook for us." So I quit.

Charlie Bellis:
Haida children were brought into the school when Charlie was in grade seven. *"That picture at the museum of the school class—one of the first integrated schools in BC. The province banned Native people from going to their schools for years and years. They needed the pupils to open the high school [in New Masset]."*

GROWING UP IN NEW MASSET

Percy used to be real cute when he's born. He got a long hair. It's all wavy. Johnny was like that. My Johnny. When they're born, they keep on combing his hair back and it grow just rolling up. That's the way Johnny's was. He had a long hair for quite awhile. Till one day, he was walking home.

Somebody said, "Where's your curly hair, boy?"

"Momma cut them off."

Johnny Bellis, Nora's son:
"It was tough. We were pretty poor. And cold winters. Oh, the summers were great. I always remember trout, just down on the dock, bullhead fishing, trout fishing. She was sure a good mother. Always had lunch on the table when I came home from school.

"I took my mother out deer hunting one time. I can't remember the name of the meadow. So I was calling deer, blowing on the spear of grass. A bear came running toward us. I was so brave I took off running. I looked back. She was a hundred feet behind me. She was just flat out running.

"In Jordan River we had a large picture on the wall. It was green with trees and a waterfall. We were so proud of it. We went into Victoria one night. Naanii was visiting us and baby-sitting. She thought the picture looked too bare, and decided to fix it. So she glued several pictures of deer on it that she cut out of a book."

Dick Bellis, Nora's son:

"She pushed every one of us through grade twelve. The older I get, the more I realize how wise the old woman was.

"They were happy days. Go out for the tide, dig clams, find crab traps, stop and fish for trout in the river, then shoot a deer on the way in. It took us three trips to bring all the stuff out that time. Every 24th of May we'd walk out there to Bluejacket to go swimming. Of course it was warmer. We'd stay there the next three months.

"We lived on the water. We dove in the water from the docks. We could catch a dime before it hit the bottom. We'd get up at five; go clam digging. Come back and go to school. Second tide, we'd dig again. If we weren't doing that, we worked in the cannery. It was cold. You could eat any crab with broken legs.

"We all drove old jalopies. We didn't lack for food and fun. It was a good place to grow up. We lacked nothing. A loving mother. We didn't have a dad, but all the other dads taught us, Burton, Hageman, bowline knots, how to skin a deer.

"We were busy every day. The cannery was here, so in the morning, we could get a big fish head, put it on the hook and hang it off the dock. At lunchtime or supper, we'd pull up a nice thirty-to forty-pound halibut.

"There were three sets of brothers growing up, Morrison brothers, Hageman brothers and the Bellis brothers. We would go hunting up the slough, and we'd sit, three sets of brothers, and get the evening flight. We'd get our limit. Six young men, six automatic rifles. Then we'd walk to the Chown, do the same thing.

"I never discovered racism till I left the Islands to go to vocational training school. I left home in '56 so Mother moved uptown in 1954. [126] Of course it was still bush."

Danny Bellis, Nora's grandson:
"I remember staying with Nora at the Main Street house. Had a heyday looking through all her goodies, playing the gramophone. Someone had shot a bear right beside the house. First time I saw a bear hung and skinned."

SAM

Sam Simpson saw a description of a new kind of crab trap in the *Pacific Fisherman*: "rugged heavy traps [that] would stand up to the wave action in shallow water. I got Fred Bellis to come from Masset and help us make up similar traps with his gas welding outfit."[127]

You know what happened? About twenty years ago I guess. Maybe twenty-four. I live right across the police station. And I never was out on the beach for ages. And Patty Setso came up. I said, "Pat, let's go out clam digging. We'll get five boxes each. We going to show them how to do it." And I never was out on the beach since I was young. You know what we get? We did get five boxes each. It must be lots of clams anyway. And we sold them.

And payday there's a great big cheque for me. They give me one of Kenneth Bell's son's cheque, by mistake. I told somebody.

I said, "Just keep it. See what happen." And two or three days I had lots of money from the cannery for the clams. We got five boxes each. And somebody, over one hundred dollars. They real good diggers, those.

Sam Simpson grew up around his dad's canneries, at Naden Harbour, Tow Hill and New Masset, and was a cannery man all his life. In 1950, he and his wife Jessie built a cannery in New Masset, processing fish, crab and clams. Courtesy of Sam L. Simpson, *The Cannery Managers*

One day there's a phone call. You know, we had the phone that you wind it up. It was Sam Simpson. He said, "Nora, I got something to tell you. They give you one of Bell's paycheque to you, in your name."

I said, "Who said that?"

"Well, yours is just five box, and there's some more there. The one that sent the cheque out, mistake it."

"Sam," I said. "It was in my name. You can damn well go to hell," I said. "I spent the whole works already," I said. I just fooled him.

"Nora," he said, "if I'm going to hell, I'll be seeing you down there too." I laugh and laugh. That's quite cute.

He didn't ask again. But I have to return it.

Massett Canners, Old Massett, circa 1926. The cannery was sold to Nelson Brothers in 1930. In 1940 Sam Simpson moved the Naden Harbour cannery to Old Massett to can crab and clams. It was closed due to rising wartime costs. H.B. Phillips and Betty Dalzell Collections, Haida Gwaii Museum, Ph03857

Sam Simpson, Naden Harbour crab cannery:

"A number of Haida families came from Masset, the men to fish the crabs and the women to pick and pack the crabmeat. The fishing gear, an iron ring with a bag of netting attached, with a buoyline up to the surface, was cheap and effective. In addition the sleek, fourteen-foot, double-ended boats, which the Haida used for hand trolling, were ideal for this kind of crab fishing. Canoe building out of a cedar log was now long past. Somewhat along the same lines as the canoe the Haida were now building these carvel-built craft with yellow cedar ribs and light red planking... using the woods that are native to our islands and sawn lumber milled by themselves. The Haida have an extraordinary ability for working with wood. In the small village of Masset there were a score and more of men, who could build these boats for their own use and for use of others in the village. Craftsmen like Robert Davidson, Robert

Beached double enders, 1919. The boats known as double enders, developed by Haida craftsmen, were incredibly important to the local fishery, for crabbing especially. According to Sam Simpson, the unique design meant double enders "were made to row" but could also be "quickly converted to sail like a bird." Harland I. Smith photo, Canadian Museum of History, 2011-0036-1409-Dm

Williams, Joe Edgars and many others. Their names should be remembered. Unfortunately it is already a lost art.

"These boats were made to row. With two men at the oars, one forward and pulling, one sitting aft and facing forward, they appeared to slide through the water with effortless ease. They were beamy and could carry a good load of fish or household goods. With bow and stern shaped almost identically they could land in a surf on our flat beaches without the danger of a wave breaking over a square stern. In a fair wind they were quickly converted to sail like a bird, with a mast held up by a hole in the forward thwart and a sprit sail made of flour sacks sewn together. I have seen them in the old days, coming down from North Island in a stiff westerly, the old lady sitting amidships placidly knitting or sewing, the old man sitting aft smoking his pipe and steering with an oar, a picture of efficiency and satisfaction. These were the boats and

the men that ushered in, in Naden Harbour, the first crab fishing on the Charlottes."[128]

ANDREW YORKE

Andrew Yorke is the only boy my auntie [Gertie] had, and he was born on one of the great big steamer boat going to Victoria. That's what they used to say. John Yorke—that was Andrew Yorke's dad. He is a union man, I guess. He fell in a hatch in Rupert, great big lumber boat. He fell in it, die right away.[129]

Andrew's uncle is my own dad. Andrew was just a spoiled boy. One day Dad was walking down and here Andrew had a wheelbarrow with a little pup. He playing with his pup. Right where Arnold got his house built down on the waterfront there.

He like to see the pup swim back. He keep on throwing the dog in the water. When the dog come up, he was loving the dog up and then he threw him down again, swim back. The little pup get tired and he got drown.

So he put him on the wheelbarrow and wheeling him home. And when Dad met him: "What's wrong with your dog, Andrew?" His name was Guud, Guud i'waans, that little boy. "What's wrong with your dog, Guud?"

"Don't you dare to wake my little pup up, Uncle. He's sleeping."

He's too little. He thought the dog was sleeping, see. He went and drown him. That's Andrew.

After he grow up I was down there visiting my mom. My dad was quite old. He feel the heat from the stove. He turns around and he bump into the railing. He did that so many times I start to laugh. It made Andrew mad. That's his own uncle. As soon as I see Andrew mad at me, it make me laugh more. Here Dad turns around and he bump into the door. I laugh so much.

My husband just got a new wristwatch. I went bump into where Dad keep on bumping and I broke the really expensive wristwatch. Andrew said, "It serves you right." I laugh so hard. I never forget it.

THE JAILHOUSE

I look after the girls when they put them in there. Charlie's wife got that job for me, watching girls when the girls go in the jail.

Down Massett, when I was kid, there's a jailhouse there, a little log cabin, real tough looking one. There's some Indian policemens. It's Charlotte Marks's dad was the policeman. Ethel [Jones]'s grandfather. And somebody else too. I can't remember who it was.

They threw them in when they drunk or fighting or things like that. And they give them so many months. They work for their fine. Why they don't do that nowadays?

They build great big wide road out to North Beach. When we were kids we used to go and play in the big road. So the big road been there till just lately, grown over with some salmonberry bushes there.

And when they threw them in jail they make them work real hard. But nowadays, they don't. I was across there. They put boys in jail. They just stay in jail, do nothing.

Even down in Victoria I guess. Father used to tell us. I remember it. There's one man. They put him in jail and he got great big heavy lead ball on his chain. He's chained down. But he could walk. They're working and dragging that. That's punishment. They call it hard labour, you know.

Down in the basement. That's where they keep them, where the tide comes in on them too. That's when somebody kills somebody. Before they hang them.

There's one man they put in and he keep practicing. And he didn't try to run away at first. He's getting stronger as he practicing. He had a good chance to exercising, hey. Keep him healthy. Then he ran away.

He went quite far and somebody says to the policeman, "He's going to run away on you."

"No. He comes right back."

He go far as one mile. Next day he go to two miles.

And one of the men said, the policemans I guess, "He's going to run away."

"No, he been do that for months, but he comes right back."

And then he pick up this thing [the ball and chain] and he walk back home.

"Oh he'll be coming back soon."

Here when he's quite far, about five miles, he got something to cut that chain off and he cut and run away. They didn't get him back because when they do that they don't go after them again. There's a rule that could be free. That's in Victoria in olden days.*

THE MARTINS

Clarence Martin:
"We saw very little of the Indian people. The Indian Agent didn't allow white people on reserve unless they stopped at his place for a special permit. And not at all after dark, 7:00 p.m. And they were a close-knit family.

---

* Maureen asked if the man was Haida. Nora replied, "Yeah, he was."

"They'd invite the whole village of New Masset, to a concert and banquet.

"Their word was their bond. You could always depend on them."

One time, Dickie was down at UBC. And he want to come home; he sent for money. He's bad enough, but he said he want to bring his partner up. I think I send seventy-five dollars down.

And right away, he was the boss at the [Juskatla logging] camp. One day there's a cheque come in, seventy-five dollars to me. I keep that. And that was bad enough, Louie Widen stop at the front of my

James Martin's son, Clarence, with his wife Phyllis. The Martins were a prominent family in New Masset and friends with Nora. Clarence ran the post office, hydro plant and fuel oil business.
Dixon Entrance Maritime Museum

place there and give me another seventy-five dollars. By mistake, they sent me two cheques.

So I went up to—Phyllis Martin was living yet. I said, "Phyllis, I got lots of money. I'm going to take a trip. I'm going to buy something real good." She look at the cheque. I told her what happened. I said, "I'm going to keep it."

"Oh no, Nora," she said. "Send it back. Whatever what you want to buy, I'll get it for you. Send this back." I think she buy me a dress or something like that. She used to buy dresses for us because we were in the choir up here. Patty Setso and me. That's Clarence's wife. She bought dresses for us.

Clarence said, "There's a teacher here. Everybody hate him and they make him real miserable." And one day the teacher come in and told Phyllis about, everybody hate him so much here. "I want to go home but I got no money." You know what Phyllis did? She sent him home. They're from old country, someplace. That's what Clarence told us.

Phyllis Martin used to be real good. She's real Christian. I start to Sunday school teacher with her for a while. Not too long. I got too much to do at home.

Clarence Martin and his dad got a big store. It burned down one time. When I live right across here then. One night his store burned down. And a few years after that his mother was alone. He got two boarders. They make homebrew upstairs in the room, had a lamp underneath the homebrew. The lamp must have fall and catch on fire. She lost all great big house with all the expensive things in there. That's Clarence's mother. His dad died before that.

CHAPTER 11

We should understand proper way

NAANII AND TSINII BROWN

In the 1940s the Browns' home still sat in the shadow of the hill that older memories name G̲ad G̲aywaas. It was set back now, fenced, with a path leading up to the house between patches of raspberry canes and strawberries.

Russell Samuels, Eliza's grandson, remembered sitting in the kitchen: "[We'd be] around that round table from the schooner. Outside back of the house was a root cellar, near as high as this room, with a shack over it, to store potatoes, carrots, turnips. They'd have vegetables pretty near year round. Across from the house were two garages, Andrew's and Joe Weir's, for their Model Ts."

Frank Collison:

"I remember it smelled like dry fish. They used to hang halibut up on racks in the kitchen. Every kitchen had a rack to dry clothes on. She always put out something to eat. We used to pack wood, Archie and I, for a nickel, up from the beach. The house was quite a ways back.

"That's the first time I really heard Haida songs sung. Andrew Brown. The first time I really heard an Indian drum. You could hear it from outside.

"He was an excellent storyteller. That's where Percy got it from. Sometimes he'd tell it the way Percy told it—he'd pull your leg a bit."

Charlie Bellis:

"We used to go visit them on Sunday. We'd walk down there when I was small. They'd put a big pot of clam and seaweed chowder in the middle of the table at mealtime. And buns and fried bread. Everybody had big horn spoons to eat with. They smelled like Indian—fish.

"They were old then. Naanii Brown was his second wife and she was a girl when Andrew was first married. They were still going out fishing then, but not doing well. Teddy went out with them, on the Ruth G.

"They had a big strawberry garden in their yard. They always were out food gathering. They food-gathered right up to the last day. Naanii Brown was really old, coming down the inlet in a rowboat.

"They talked about the time they were up the Ain dog salmon fishing. Before the end of the month it was snowing. They had to come home in the snow. They were just in rowboats. They liked rowboats. Everybody in the village had rowboats.

"My grandfather carved all year and then he went to sell them."

Mary Ann Bellis and Jean Schubert:

"Our grandparents' house was on Cecilia [Abrahams]'s lot, set at the back of the lot, a walkway up the centre, a fence. Robert Bennett's store was across the street.

"Inside, there were flowered covers over the couches, a grandfather clock in the front room, argillite dust. Out front, on the other side of the road, halibut on an A frame with poles across it. A 1927 Ford in the garage, that Fred Bellis would drive.

"I remember eating at Naanii Brown's. She'd have a big bowl in the middle of the table with seaweed and fish eggs. It was so good. She used to always have jams and jellies—red and black currants and raspberries in the garden. She was so wonderful. She never spoke a word of English. She was really kind."

Jean Schubert:

"She used to go picking berries. She never spoke sharp to me, except when I wandered too far. It was getting four o'clock. The wind was blowing. She had red huckleberries. She lifted the berries up and the wind blew the leaves away."

Mary Ann Bellis:

"I remember Uncle Percy. He bought me a doll when I was really small. They were really hard to come by. He was a huge man, blind toward the end, fisherman. He was sent to jail for having a stolen knife. They all went down and cried."

Charlie Bellis:

"The steamboat used to stop down here [Massett]. There was no wharf in New Masset. There were bags of clothing that stayed in the shed for months, got scattered around. Percy found the knife there, had it on his boat. Joe said it was his, and charged him. In those days all the Indians got were two years less a day, for everything, no matter what it was."

Margaret Adkins:

"I learned to understand my Haida language from Naanii and Tsinii Brown. Whenever we went to visit Massett, I would go to Naanii and Tsinii Brown's home and stay there all day. Tsinii Brown always worked on his argillite carvings by the window in the kitchen, wearing a cap with a green visor. His hands were always black with the argillite dust. Naanii Brown was always busy, working on fish, berries, canning fruit, making bread. The only time she sat down was when she made tea and set fresh bread and canned berries out to go with our tea. While I was visiting them they would speak Haida to one another, and English to me. As I listened to them speak to one another, I was able to understand what it was they were talking about. When I would finally go home I always left with gifts of canned berries.

"I remember the living room having many sofas and chairs and side tables with ornaments placed on crochet doilies. The dining room had a large china cabinet; on this was a large porcelain Chinese figure. This figure always fascinated me. I remember having dinner in this room, and I admired Tsinii Brown drinking tea by pouring it from his cup into the saucer. I could not understand why my mother would not allow me to do this.

"Tsinii Brown made many trips to Prince Rupert, selling his argillite carvings. I remember helping him pack boxes to a boat, as he was going back to Massett. He was telling me he didn't do too well; he only made $2,000 this trip. To me it was more like two million dollars.

"Tsinii always personalized his stories—it happened to him. He had a little gillnetter with bear's paws hanging on deck. He told this story:

"Chinese fellow said, 'Good bear paw. I buy it from you.' Tsinii, 'You buy me a bottle of whiskey, you can have it.' Chinese returned next day. 'Bear paw no good, no good.' Tsinii, 'Whiskey no good, make me sick.'"

YAAN SABLII

Russell Samuels recalled travelling with his great-grandparents, Andrew and Susan Brown, in the 1940s and '50s.

On getting seaweed at Straie Island, Gwaay t'uuwans:
"For trade not for money. Trade seaweed and dried halibut for grease. No money in it. It's all trade around.

"You gotta have the southeast, blowing like a son of a gun. Just put up the sail, one sail. Take us out there so fast. If we didn't have the wind, I'd have to row. About that much [six inches] of freeboard, with all their junk. I hated the big feather mattress. It took up most of the room.

"All by myself, but in my glory, with the dogs, and with the crows. The crows would be nice and quiet. Soon as I climb up, I'd have to see how many eggs are in the nest. The whole island was mad at me. Naanii Brown would call out in Haida to leave the crows alone.

"The place used to be loaded up with orchids [ladyslipper]. You can smell that island on a real nice day."

On his way to the Yakoun River, Russell would be in the bow, pulling on the oars, and Andrew further back, pushing on the oars:*
"Two days. Camp at Nadu. Take off the feather mattress. Pack it back on the boat. I used to hate that. The only thing they left behind is the house. Everything else they take. I hate packing that stuff.

"Next morning, he had the tide all figured out. No rush, no hurry, slowly put things back in the boat. Give me time to fool around with my dog. He figured it would take six hours to Yakoun. Sure enough, six hours and we'd be coming into camp, with two dogs and the grandmother's cat. Grandmother's cat was always pregnant. I used to look forward to going there, for a lot of trout fishing.

"They used to make bannock a different way, called it Yaan sablii. In a fry pan, no lid. Make baking powder bread, thick. The way they used to do it—bake it on the outside, slow heat, till it's brown outside, raw inside. After, take it from the fire, a couple feet away if you've got a good fire. Stand it up. Not too big a fire so it burns. Don't cut it. Break it off, soak it with butter—the real butter that you could taste.

"Everyone lived great then. Pretty near everyone had an orchard, red currants, black currants, gooseberries, raspberries, inside along the fence, turnips, potatoes.

"K'aayang was where the orchard was, two types of plums, red and green, apple trees, lots of cherry. The last place where the poles were."[130]

---

* There are two different Haida words for the two rowing styles. Haida Elder and language teacher Tsinii Stephen Brown said, according to Jaalen Edenshaw's understanding, that older men generally rowed facing forward; younger people rowed facing backward, Western style.

THE FLOOD

Matt and Leila Abrahams had a troller and lived down the street from Nora. Leila and Nora often visited. When he was a teen, Matt, Eliza's son, once swam ashore from his uncle's boat, anchored at North Island, to go to a dance.
Collection of the author

Leila Abrahams:

"It was him [Andrew Brown] I heard it from. You never listen I guess. He talk about the anchor.

When the flood came even the great big mountains went under, and this little hill here was the only one. Telephone Hill,* that's the only one that was sticking out, so they tied up.[131]

"And they said they had an anchor made out of things that you could shape and it was yellow. And they all anchored up on Telephone Hill.

"When the flood start going down, they run out of water. They didn't have no place to get water. And two boys, they said it was bubbling.

"So they cut one of the canoes and they went to see it. Something was bubbling right out, right back here. So they got their water from there, till it went right down. And when the water went right down, they cut the cedar bark lines what they use to tie the boat up.

"And they left all those chunks of yellow things there. That was gold."

Nora: Every year the gold goes further down.

---

* Telephone Hill is part of a ridge southeast of New Masset.

Leila: And it was this water we're drinking now. That's why he said not to go picking berries up here, 'cause there's a bottomless pit there. He said never to go. There's a hole there, it's got no bottom, just water. That's where we getting our town water from.

Seems like the ones that survived was those that anchored up at Telephone Hill, and they started over again after the flood. They had to start all over again. The ones that were alive. So there must have been people here before the flood.

And after the flood when they were starting over again, they saw something come up the inlet there. They went to see it and it was a totem pole. That's where they got the idea of totem poles.

Nora: They look underneath, in the waters, the water was just full of totem poles. They never had totem poles before. They copy that. Underneath the water, totem poles. ·

Leila: I guess they weren't even scared. They think it was a miracle or something. To learn something from there I guess. So they just copied.

FEED STRANGER PEOPLE

All the people used to tell how to respect other people. Young ones have to learn how to respect older people. I remember my grandparents keep on telling us how to respect other people, or else they never respect us.

I got a real old granny and grandfather. I used to listen to them. The most thing they used to tell us is feed strangers. And that's just the way the bible says too, feed anybody with what you can spare and that's what I try to do. And I got so many friends here. There's nothing like welcome strangers.

Sometimes stranger people look real proud. "If they want to be proud they can stay in their own home, in their land." That's what my grandfather used to say. If you want to be friends with other people, just go out and be mix with them.

Our real old grandmother and grandfather, so they used to know everything. In my young days, they wouldn't let us eat sea urchins. Great-great-great-grandmother poisoned from sea urchins. I don't supposed to eat sea urchins. You never be rich.

Soon as girls get up, they pick up all the dirt from the ground. They bound to be rich when they grow up, to keep themselves neat, and you'll live long time too.

So anybody can do that. If they listen to their granny. Makes a long life, and real wisdom, see. What about King Solomon? He didn't ask for long life. He didn't ask for getting rich. All he did was ask for wisdom. And God give him everything else—wisdom, richer, long life. And he's the only king that was live longer and real rich.

They used to call something in the air. That's the way mother and grandmother and them used to. Something, a spirit in the air. That's what they believe. The spirit in the air, a ghost or something, punish you if you do something wrong. That's what they used to say, they said. They're scared too.

They pray to the same god. I mean, my grandfather used to say, they call it "something in the air." How could we say in English now? Something that's in the air. They knew there's something in the air anyway. And they didn't want to do anything in wrong because of the thing in the air is some kind of good spirit.[132]

And then they knew there's a bad spirit too. That's the one, a bad spirit. Make you do things wrong. That's what I heard my grandfather used to say. You have to be on the right spirit.

When they were eating, the fire make noise like *booo*. The ghost people want something to eat. It used to hurt their feelings when that happen and they were eating good food. Whatever you eat you put [some food] in fire right away.

They used to say the blessing for the food since that time, since they brought the gospel here. That's around maybe 1870 something, when the preacher came here. That's quite old. My grandfather was believe in it so much. My grandfather and my grandmother and my mother and my dad.

Time before, they believe in, to be good my mother and my grandfather used to believe in feeding strangers. Give food to strangers. What my grandfather always tell us, if you eating, if somebody comes in, don't let him sit there, give him whatever you eat in front of him right away, because they seen it.

Somebody come in, in a place where everybody's eating, and they pull out seat for him and he's sitting there. Here he fall back and die right there. They said he's starved to death. People were eating so much and they didn't offer him anything.

That's a great big lesson, my grandfather. So anybody come around, give them tea right away these days he said. It says in the bible feed another one all the time. And that's why. They didn't hear it from the bible but they're born with it like.

Feed somebody else. My dad is like that. He like to feed stranger people. It doesn't matter if he don't know them. If they're stranger, be sure and give them cup of tea right away.

RESPECT ANY FOOD

We have to respect any food that God give it to us, not to call filthy. That's good word, eh? *Ee*, you don't supposed to say that. Everything God give it to us, for us to clean it and eat it. So we can't call it filthy things. We were told and told. I got a real old grandmother and grandfather used to tell us, "Don't call anything filthy." If it's not clean it's up to you to clean it and eat it.

There's a heaven, and all kinds of animals on there, and God sent them down to the earth. And they hear something. "Take those and kill one for your people to eat it." His name, it's in the bible. "Kill one of them and eat it." And this man on the earth says, "I don't eat things that not clean. I don't eat it."

And then the whole thing turns right up. You can see that. God sent everything down for us to eat, for us to kill and eat it, but when that man said, "I don't eat unclean things," so God took the whole works back to heaven again.

So right today, we can't say, if anything to eat, don't say it's a filthy thing. God takes things away. You understand that. I heard that when I was just a child, and it stays in my—I don't supposed to say, "Not clean enough to eat it." Everything belongs to God. God sent those down for us to eat it. We can't call it filthy things.

I hope you understand everything.

> One time there's a boy,
> got spunky.
> They're eating fish
> and he wouldn't eat with his parents.
> So he chew one for a long, long time
> and then he, on the beach, sand, where there's water,
> he spit this fish out and then he buried it.
> He went and take a look at it.

Great big dried fish, all soaked.
And he was so hungry,
he just look at and he died.
He starved to death.

If anybody get spunky, wouldn't eat dinner, they tell us that story.

They always tell us what to do. I remember my grandmother and granddad would say to us if you want to eat something, don't keep telling your parents or your brother. If they go and get it, something might happen.

That's why they told us not to tell others what we want to eat. This person would go and get it; something might happen. So if you want anything, don't say nothing about it. They already knew you want it.

CHARLIE'S DOG

I never had a dog. Charlie and his wife, Chubby, had one. It's a black Labrador. One day I went. Charlie's wife was working in a cannery. There's a big bag of clothes. I take a sweater and hang it up on the line, my clothesline.

I come out and the sweater's not there. Where could it go? I go to the house and the dog has brought it right back where I got it.

So I take it back and hang it up again. Same thing happens.

The third time he was putting it on the floor and he was laying down on it.

UP BEHIND THE CATHOLIC CHURCH[133]

About the school time, they used to bring big bag of clothes, you ordered for, for the kids. While Fred and Ralph Stafford were talking, talking, while they talking, the dog pack all the clothes out. Big parcel from Eaton's.

He turns around. "Nora, let Ralph Stafford see the clothes that I bought for the boys today." We couldn't find it. Our place is just small. Big bag of the suit for going to school. It was right by the table, on the floor.

"Where did you put it Nora?"

I said, "I didn't put it away." And the dog was sitting there, sitting right close to his master.

And that man look at the dog. "Now, what did you do with his clothes?" .

The dog run out to the Catholic church way. So that old man is walking up after him. "Get the kids' clothes. They need it." He dig. The dog buried the whole thing. I think that was the cutest thing. Pack the clothes up behind the Catholic church.

IN OLDEN DAYS

In olden days they told us not to treat any dog [badly that] belongs to somebody else. Be nice to any animal. We used to listen to our parents not to treat anybody else dog mean.

When I was little, my grandfather and them used to talk about, there's a man that's real sick. I think he got TB or something. They used to put lean-to on the house, and the sick man stays there. They don't allow them to stay in the longhouses. If anybody sick, they used to be so scared of it. Really scared, just like it's poison. A lean-to for mother and baby. If a man's sick, he's outside.

One day—he had a dog, his pet. Here the dog was just outside the sick man's door. Door was open. And there's a man come around and kick his dog, real hard. He got the gun right by him, where he's laying down. "Kick my dog again, I'll shoot your head off."

He got real scared. That was real good. Something to learn. But I think they make the story more dangerous to us kids. They used to tell us the man shoot that man's head off. It wasn't, I don't think. "Just kick my dog again, I'll shoot your head off." And here they used to tell us he did. But I don't think it's true.

So they told us not to treat anybody's pet, not a dog, because if you get killed, if he shoot you, well, they couldn't do a thing about it.

INDIAN MEDICINE

I was quite sick. And I went to see the doctor. And you know what he said? He looks at me and he said, "Now what's wrong with you lady?"

I tried to explain.

"There's nothing wrong with you. All you have to do, young lady—quit drinking and quit smoking. You will be all right." And he got paid for that.

I feel like swear at. I can say, "You goddam horse-ass doctor. I don't drink and I don't smoke." But good thing I keep my mouth shut. He died long time ago. He smoke too much I guess. He's a traveller. He come here to tell me to quit smoking.

My mother said if any sickness I was the only one stay with the medicine. I don't know why. I just want to try to be good and take the medicine on time. She said that's why I pull through all the time. I got the measles and some other sickness going on. It didn't even stay with me mother said. I take the medicine, right on time all the time so. Crazy way to want to live, hey?

Leila Abrahams:

"I was born down North Island, 1916 [fishing season, July 12] and my dad took me back to register me in Alaska 'cause he wasn't under the Indian Act. That's why I got the land claim so easy, 'cause I was registered over there.

"I heard this story from Andrew Brown. Fur seals were so expensive and when you going to start hunting for it you drink all kinds of medicine, and eat it raw, forty sticks you eat, and then you don't drink water. He said he ate twenty; didn't even know what happened to him. He found himself by the river and he was trying to drink water, but he went back and he ate the other twenty.

"When it's time to go hunting, he said it was nothing to shoot that fur seal. It was real hard to get it. I guess they were getting scarce. But when you shoot them, when you go over and pick it up, he said bubbles would be coming out from the mouth. He said that's from all the Indian medicine you've been eating and drinking.

That's all."

That Indian medicine cleans your stomach out and at the same time they used to believe it give you good luck. You can easily believe it. When you feel sick you can't do nothing, hey; when you're feeling well you can do anything.

So that medicine is the ones that heals your stomach, cleans you out and make you feel like work all the time. That's why they so active after they take it so many months and they give you good luck. That's what my grandmother and them used to say. Your body is all cleaned out; your system all cleaned out. And you don't sick and you feel like working all the time.

The one that take that medicine volunteer, just like it says. Early to bed and early to rise, healthy and wealthy and wise. That's just the way that thing work.

I think they get them anytime. From here [elbow to knuckle]. And they boil them just the way they are. They don't scrape them out. And then you strain it when you going to drink it. That's what my dad and my grandmother and them used to say.

All the prickles are all cooked. And some people scrape that off. Scrape the needles off. With a potato peeler these days, it's real easy. Just scrape them off and be sure they count the sticks.

They get about forty. There's a name for it in Haida. Ten, they had name for it. Each ten. Forty of them. Forty of the sticks. That's why it's easy to pack it home I guess.

They call it in Haida the forty is limit for medicine. Drink it three times a day. Just like those other medicine, as long as you're inside. They used to take it when they got a real bad disease.

They could smell from your skin, and then when the smell goes, the sickness left. That's what they used to say. You smell like medicine, and then when it leave, when you get healed, all the smell goes off. That's why you could tell that you got healed. So that's the way my grandmother and them used to tell us.

MIDWIFE OIL

Kind of oil, but I think more like seal oil in the olden days.

Maureen: She would put her hands in seal oil?

Nora: Keep her hands real warm for a long time. Her hands get so soft.

Mrs. Nix, Mrs. Nix from Hydaburg. That's Leila's mother-in-law. She died long time ago. Quite old—she turned the [breach] baby around. And somebody got a blanket, cloth. She just go like this [squeeze]. They said they couldn't even feel her hand. Just go like this and all the big clot of blood comes out. That's all.

ARTHRITIS

The only medicine I know is when anybody got arthritis so bad. In Skidegate they use this medicine. The bark of it, they scrape it off. And they boil it and they drink it. More the better from it. We call it grey berries, a wild one.

The berries they eat them. They make a good jam. And the bark. Maude [Moody] and them just tell me more the better from it. She think it was cancer too she heal. From that time everybody use it up there.

There's some up at Bluejacket. That's where we used to pick for jam.

PITCH

They put pitch and some kind of herb with it and they stuck it on there until there's a great big roots would come out. It maybe sounds like cancer. Nobody used to have cancer down there.

They used to say they stuck it on the sore and even when you're paining someplace, you stuck it on, whatever it is it draws it out. And whatever was around there, round ball with lots of legs on like. Sounds like cancer, hey. And the inside would be round and then white legs, million of them.

Some people when this big thing comes out, everybody used to go and see it. They call it boil, gugstl'agaaw, you know, and they put pitch on. They never take it off till it start to bring even the leg off the boil. Even Dr. Deagle heard that. He was telling me about it. They said they let it stick on there, never touch it till it draws that sickness out, the whole. Sometime big thing come, slide out.

And I think I seen a hole in where it comes out. I can't remember who it was. I was just a kid. They always talk about it so much. How they call it. They had different name for the body of the thing. More like look like spider to me that's what, great big legs on it, white.

After my husband [died], I kick on into a nail and I was suffering with that for nine months. I was making a closet and I run into great big spike sticking out. Right here. Nine months. Soon's I eat little bit butter, it runs. Pus running out. I have to do without butter, anything with oil in it makes it run. And I go to a choir practice and this thing gets so stink, and I feel out of place. So I think I quit going there.

Nine months I suffered with this, till Dickie, my boy, "Johnny let's go up and look for pitch for Mom. She's too cranky because she's too sick."

And they got lots of pitch for me in a can. So I fix it up. I put on brown paper and put that. I strained it. You get it warm, it start to get soft. And just plain. They said they stick it on one time but I did it opposite way. Every fifteen minutes I pulled that out, and threw this one away. Put another one on. In four days' time this get better. You could see it start to healing. You know, it get better real fast.

SORE EYE

Teabag on your eye all night. Wake up; your eye is foggy, then better.

WATER

Olden days, when they're taking medicine they don't supposed to drink water. It's unlucky they used to say. But now we have to drink lots. Get yourself all cleared out. That's different. But in olden days they don't supposed to drink water at all, just the medicine that they take. Isn't that funny? We don't supposed to drink water if you want to get the medicine work on the sickness. Sure enough, they never used to have any kind of sickness at all.

PORRIDGE

For maybe twenty years I just eat porridge, brown sugar, lots of milk. And I don't have trouble at all. As long as somebody's stomach is clean, you're healthy. I'm scared to eat meat. Chicken is all right, but meat—it's stuck in your stomach.

CLAMS

Now you might get some clams out there. You clean the clams. Don't touch the little foot part. They're soft enough, but—the necktie they call it. And the head, the black thing, just cut the black off. Not more than that; you just waste it then. And you chopped it up real good. And boil it. And put seaweed in it. And you can boil potatoes. Eat it with the potatoes just like meat. That keeps you healthy.

SEAWEED

That's worth million dollar recipe—my dad is a drunkard. Every time when he's hangover, he always tell mother to boil seaweed for him. Every time. Mother would doctor him up right away. And he was old when he die. That's what Leila said. "You going to live like Tsinii Brown," she said. "Oh I'm old enough now," I said. "I don't want to live that long."

SPEAK FOR YOURSELF

You have to talk for yourself. If you don't they step on you.

I remember when I was young, I notice that they don't invite old ladies out for dinner, just their husbands. I don't know why. You have to keep on pounding in their ears.

If you worry about something, just hit the great big spike [hit the nail on the head]. That's what they think I did one time. When they had a big meeting, about the Co-op. When trying to get people to start the Co-op. They said—everything you buy, 10 percent off.

[I said,] "And I never get anything 10 percent off yet."

There's a verse says, "Ask and it shall be given to you; seek and he shall find; knock and it shall be opened unto you." Nobody know the truth, but we have to find it yourself.

[I asked,] "What did you think of my speech tonight?"

Mr. Taylor said, "Pretty good."

PUT US TOGETHER; THEN YOU GOT A VOICE

Every morning when I build the fire and when it start to go, if it's scattered over, you have to poke it and put it together and it start to go. That's the way life is. We have to be together. Amen.

When I open the door, red cedar—*pik pik pik pik*, just like an old lady squawking. Like alder tree just keep quiet and burning away, and you have to put even the one that's squawking, "Come in," and it burns. Isn't that true? Put them together, and burn. You can say Amen.

I see so many people do things wrong. That just hurt me. They do things to me, so awful. Like I don't cook fancy. As long as something keep you healthy. Even cooking, they want to beat another one. That's not the way.

Christian life is just like building a fire. If you want the fire to go on, just put them together, it started. But if you don't touch it, it just going to black out.

See the fire. You build a fire, it's all scattered, no power in it. If you put us together, then you got a voice. Amen.

If you ask somebody to go to church, it was just like four steps go to heaven, L-O-V-E. If you don't, you go right down. If you don't cause somebody go to church, if you don't care for them, you don't know what way she's going, down or up. Just four letters, you keep going up, going up, going up. L-O-V-E, four steps to heaven.

That's what Pentecostal always do—"I love you." That's the biggest word that you can say to somebody else. Lift them up. Lift them up in your heart. You feel lighter because everybody loves you too. I can say Amen.

If anybody tell you things too, some gossiping even. They tell their friends. There's two way of gossiping—somebody hate them [or] some of them, they love them and tell them, tell them what's wrong ahead of the time.

If you tell somebody what's right, just be kind to everybody. You got reward for it that your sins are forgiven. Ten times more than what you done on this earth. You have reward coming yet from heaven.

All you want is to be happy and love everybody. That lifts you up. Here I overlook that. Soon's I tell the kids what I want, they send me big boxes of stuff what I ask for. God will do the same thing, if I'm not shamed of what I want.

I try to keep away from earthly doings, like when they're doing big things they always call on me. My throat went haywire. That's the only thing I depend on, my voice. My voice been taken away. My ears been taken away. Now my eyes start to—it's real foggy on this side. The only time I feel quite all right is when I'm knitting away. Sometimes they buy it; sometimes it's something needed. I give it. I don't pray for money but it comes to me.

I'm always happy, because Teddy used to tell me, "Mom, if I do good for other people, two or three times a day, make me feel real good." To help others, that's Teddy.

I have to tell you about my life when I go through all this sickness. All I do is pray, just keep on praying. But one worth that helps me quite a bit, is I can do all things through Christ, which strengthens me. That's all I used to think of it when I'm too sick to think about anything else. It takes two or three together in his name, and you ask for thing. If you want to be healed, take two or three together in his name, and he answer that. That's the only ones that I used to believe.

And I used to think I hope I can get somebody to be with me and pray, but there was nobody around in the hospital like that. I used to wish I can have just one person more to pray with me, because it says in the bible, there's two or three together in his name. It was the same way with these days, if you need something so bad from the government, it seems like that, just the way the bible is. It takes two or three together in his name, and ask for it and God helps you, and answer the prayer.

Dear heavenly father, give us the wisdom to write the story of our life. Put it in the book; we can put in it. Maureen, bless her with wisdom, understanding other people, and let us help others too. If we help other people, we get blessing for it. Thank you for the wisdom for Maureen and the work. Give us the health. All we need is the health. In the name of Our Lord Jesus, bless our book too. Amen.

FEEL OUT OF PLACE

I'm trying to wash my pants out, and Isabella Smith her name was. She was my best pal. If I don't tell her to do something for me she feel out of place. She told me herself.

And then next one was Andrew. My grandson was over at the lodge. And his uncle keep on telling the other boy who was with him, and he didn't say anything to Andrew, didn't tell him to do nothing. What hurts me is, Andrew can't say that to his uncle, "Why don't tell me to do something?"

He just tell that other boy, Godfrey Kelly's son. "Naanii," he said, "Uncle Ted don't even tell me to do something for him."

Make him feel out of place. So I told Teddy. But it's pretty hard for me to make him understand it. Till I tell him the background. But now I think he's going to. This last year I told him to talk to Andrew. Tell him to do something so make him feel at home.

If I don't tell her to do nothing. Feel out of place. That's just the way it is. I used to feel that way. It's hard to explain to somebody else. So you girls remember that.

BORN FOR SOMETHING

Tell the children what to do. Make their children work for their bread and butter so they would understand it. They know how to. Not waiting for government to feed them. They can easily earn their living. Lots of kids are real smart. Find it out, what you born for.

So many people are born for something. They don't try it. They don't try to get what they're born for. They can't be good for nothing lifetime. They're bound to be born for something. That's what my dad used to say and my grandfather.

So many people are born for something. Find it out, what you born for. Just like when I was kid, I want to find out what I was born for. First thing is music. My mother used to like music. So I start.

Nora hamming it up at the T'aalan Stl'ang Rediscovery Camp. Thom Henley photo

If you play piano you can play anything. I play violin, mandolin, banjo, accordion. I don't know the words, but the banjo knows it. I even play saxophone. Right now I'm too old to do all that. Still I get so lonesome for guitar.

Here if it wasn't for music I don't think I live this long. That keeps me going.

For young boys and girls, when they get so restless, if they got guitar then they can do that, get miserable life out of you, real easy.

Louie Widen ask me to teach his boy. "I can't give you money for the lessons, but I'll give you ride to Massett every time." I've been riding on taxi for nothing, and the boy didn't even get to know it. And I'm riding around for nothing.

Something to get your mind out of being lonesome. That's one big medicine for it, to play music.

When I was in Rupert, for five years I lived there when Andrew was baby. I was with the mens all the time, playing music in the Pentecostal church. One lesson in the bible, women don't supposed to be with mens in a crowd. If you want to be, you have to be with your husband.

"Well I got no husband," I said. "What about me? I got no husband."

"Well you couldn't help it. You can stay."

"King's Highway." Even when Teddy die.* Coming home singing that song. It helped me quite a bit. It really lift me up.

TELL THE CHILDREN WHAT TO DO

Like my grandparents used to tell us that when you're young you just like right on a steep hill, you can slide down from that if you don't keep yourself, do the right things, you slide down anytime. So it's best to do the right thing since you were young. If you try it you get it. And ask your parents to help you, to pray for you.

I like to give anybody advice because when you're young you don't know nothing on this world. What's coming; what's going. All you have to do is to get in the life that's so good. But you have to remember it's a steep hill; you're right on the top. You slide down anytime if you don't be careful.

There's a big meeting and they asked the parents to get up and tell others what you find out in your life. Since you're mother, you have to spank your kids because you love them, not because you hate them. That's all I said. So remember that. If anybody bawl the kids out, they not bawling them out because they hate

---

* Ted Bellis, Nora's son, died on April 2, 1991.

them. They love them. They didn't want to see them do things wrong. Even after you're gone, they know what to do.

That's one of the hardest things to do. How can they just depend on government to feed their children and they just go happy go lucky and what do they get? They just killing themself. The parents kill themself drinking. They never used to do that. If anybody drunk, everybody thought, "Oh he's doing something wrong," but now it's nothing.

When they get alcoholic where they going to get the drinks from? No money. People, they will talk smart. "I been living here all my life. I can do this for myself." But they can't.

That's just what it's so hard to boss older people. They old enough. And I could see they don't even tell the kids not to do that. I used to tell my boys when it's dinnertime, I told them not to do that. They never used to. Kids are real easy to train. Maybe just mine anyway. That's all they need. They just don't do that. Soon's you bawl your own kids, they take gun and shoot themselves. Get rid of themself. So they're too scared to say anything to them. All over the place I guess.

"Oh I love them too much." If I love them I didn't want them to do things wrong. I can stop them. If they don't listen, well, that's their fault, when they grow old enough. I don't feed my kids. They had to go and work for their own bread and butter. It's really up to their parents. Really.

I saw, Wilfred Bennett got a big family, hey. None of them in trouble. And the way Wilfred Bennett used to do, write a note for the kids hanging by the door. Your job is like this today and all that. Each one of them. So many girls had a work for themselves in the house.

I really, pretty tough to trying to suggest, they talk smart to you. They not happy unless they did something wrong, hey. Kids are. Like I used to hear some other boys talking: "I just feel like to beat him up." "He beat her up and then I feel all right." You know.

So really hard to suggest, when it's the parents' fault, nobody else.

Maybe it's just me that I like to please Mother and them, see, do some work, so I grow up with it, see, doing things for my mother. And my dad.

Like these days, their mother would scold the children and the children misunderstand it. They don't know their mother scold them because they didn't want them to go wrong. And they think they meant to be hate them. It wasn't the hate. You spank your own kids just to straighten their life out. And they thought, "Mother hates me." They don't.

I know, one of my boys just left the house because his brother and his dad they start to fighting. The boys start to fight and their dad get in with them. I said, "Teddy get out." Just for him to be on safe side. And he thought I meant it. He beat it away and he never come back.

Till he start to work. "Momma, I going to buy all the clothes you need and I'm gonna take you to Charlotte on a plane and then you come back, one day." Even one day I go up and come back. He kinda understand it that I didn't meant for him to be get out. I didn't want him to get hurt, when two big mens—Charlie was quite big and his dad was quite big. One against two is too much. They might hurt him.

He beat it out and never come back. I just love him so much, didn't want to cry when I tell him, so I still waiting yet to tell him. And he was gone now.

So if anybody, the young boys, if your mother scold you, she didn't mean one word of hate. It's just a love. Their mother love them; they didn't want them to get hurt.

But children just don't understand it. I start to understand it when I was over sixty years old. I just find it out. So, I was hoping it get in my mind little earlier and I could tell my children then.

I hope everybody would understand it now, because it's so hard to get to understand all that life, the way the life is.

CHECK ON YOURSELF

This is the song I always think of:

> Ask and it shall be given you,
> Seek and ye shall find,
> Knock and it shall be opened unto you.

Just search every day. Like many times I find out things when I'm searching. Like right now I'm thinking to learn how to pray the right way. The bible tells the truth. Search it yourself. Don't go by somebody else, what they tell you.

I thought I'll check on myself. I thought—I don't talk to somebody, just over phoning. I phone to somebody and they said, "What you phoning for? You get me so scared."

"Who you think phoning?"

She said, "I thought it was one of my sisters phoning. You get me scared."

It sounds real awful in Haida. So. I wasn't worthwhile having for a friend. That's just the way it sounds like. And I don't talk to her over the phone. I check on it and it was twenty-three years ago.

So when some of you people have to check on yourself and you find out lots of faults in your heart. You don't love anybody.

Naanii Nora with her grandson Andrew Bellis outside Queen Charlotte Hospital. Nora wanted the younger generations to learn from her stories. Mary Ann Bellis photo

Just check on yourself. And you find out lots of things. And ask God to forgive you for that. That's true too.

It is true. Here I don't talk to so many people. I can't talk to them. If they hurt my feelings I don't forget it. Like this, when I phoned. She said, "You get me so scared. I thought it was my sister." So I don't.

It was twenty-three years ago, when Andrew was born. That's how I know how long ago it was. That's how long I was. Real good at it.

So I'm scared to quit talking to somebody. I just keep on be friends. Smile at people and the world will smiles with you.

JUST LIKE DRIFTWOOD

Dick Bellis, 2001:
"Mother said, 'White people are just like driftwood. They drift in, they stay for awhile and then they drift on their way again.'"

And I would like to say a few words about Haidas being here. We've been happy here and we got so many friends. The ones that comes in, we welcome them. If there's anything they don't know, we would like to help them with it. There's nothing like trying to be friends with strangers. Some people think they're too proud to be friends with Haidas. But we are different people.

In olden days they used to gather the food up for winter. They smoke them, and a whole year's supply, and nobody goes hungry on this island. When there's four big tides in a month, they get enough seafood with the low tides. I never heard anybody go hard up for food in Queen Charlotte Island. Each one of us knows what to do for winter. And they get salmon—they smoke them and they dry them.

And the newcomers, when they came to this island, they're wondering what we live on. That's true enough. Looks like there's nothing around.

But when you get to know how to live in Queen Charlotte Islands, you're just like a millionaire. You got more than food gathering, and everything that's so expensive they get it for nothing on this island. As long as you can get up early, when there's low tide, it was just like a rich people. You get all the food that you need to get.

This is for the newcomers. Looks like there's nothing to eat around here. But it's different, kind of secret. Anything that we need, we go by the tide. Go away with the tide; come home with the tide. Just like time and tide waits for no man.

WE SHOULD UNDERSTAND PROPER WAY

The trees are just like god plants, everything. And when they grow up they start to destroy them. And they cut down all the best-looking ground. It's all bald-headed. So nowadays—we used to have a decent weather. Now it been like this weather for over a year now. Something that we should understand proper way. And the way we can learn is just go to church and make up what the bible says. That's all I thought it would be help.

Used to be rain all the time. But it's been dry like this for two years now. It wasn't like that before. I remember it's raining all the time. Sunshine little bit, then rain again, sunshine little bit. The weather never was like this before. We soon get to Hawaiian Island I guess.

If it wasn't for the trees this island was nothing. All the logs are taking out, million dollars. And what we get out of it? Look how many great big logs going up. Everybody else makes living out of it. What we get out of it? Nothing. The whole island is going to be finished up, the logs, all over.

Takes quite a while, the trees are growing. Look. I planted a tree twenty-one years ago. Look how small it is yet. When Andrew was born, we plant that. It's jack pine. Spruce might grow quicker.

During the war this is the only place they get the biggest timber.[134] They take it out even then, first war, great big loads of it. Mr. Edenshaw had a big place there. They log every log out of it. Henry Edenshaw's place, and Douglas Edenshaw's place. It's all logged out now they said. It's a ways from Buckley Bay. Henry Edenshaw's timber there; Douglas supposed to have it.

They think tree grows real fast. They don't. They don't grow fast. They plant them. It takes about hundred years to be useful. They're really slow.

They kind of knew it but they couldn't do a thing about it. They tried to stop them; there's nobody to help them. I know they used to have meetings and meetings. It didn't even help. Still the loggers come in, camps come in. Inlet was just full of camps, logging camps. Many, many people, taking the timber out. It's still going, just the way it was when I was kid. That's about eighty years ago. Since I was kid we used to see the logs taking out.[135] I remember when I was eight years old. I used to see that going out all the time. Logs, logs, going out. Later on, 1910 or '15, there's some more people coming in, taking logs out. The inlet was just plumb full with camps. So many loggers up here. That's all the money goes to.

They [logging companies] just wouldn't listen. They just think of the money. That's all they think about. And they didn't make few dollars, they make million dollars from that. And what do we get out of it? Nothing.

When I was just a baby, my dad was cook for the surveyors, to survey out the logs around Yakoun River, all over. For government. And Dad was saying, "We wouldn't go out surveying today. They wouldn't see us." They'd protest.

It's the logs that's like a gold mine to them. So I remember they told them not to cut logs out here. They just wouldn't listen. The man I cook for go out there and cut all the logs. Out where you stay [Tow Hill Road]. They cut it just the same, even when they try to stop them. He's the best faller, that man I cook for. He just laugh at it. He used to drink it up, but since he was here he bought a real dandy car.

It take long time they said, the ones that planting, that's for a hundred years. Who's going to live a hundred years? They wouldn't listen. Just like an animal was hungry. They just going to eat it right away, eat whatever they could.

I ALWAYS DO CRAZY THINGS

Eating alone is just like a poison. I can't even drink the tea, it tastes so rotten. Here it tastes so good when you're here, when I drink it with you.

Fred would never do without a pie. I had to cook pies every day. It's been over forty-four years I don't bake pie every day. I'm having a rest.

Cook crabs. You put baking soda in it, a spoonful of baking soda. Crab all get cleaned out. Here the one that Charlie cook them looks real dirty. I forget to tell him about it. Put spoonful of baking soda in there. Boil it. All the dirt boils right out and it's clean then. I was sorry that I didn't tell him before.

Eliza's Molasses Cake:
½ cup molasses, lots of brown sugar and lots of raisins because they can afford it. 3 eggs, about ½ cup lard, about 3 ½ cups flour, but I always mix it as long as it's black enough, and baking powder. She put lots of raisins, and nowadays you put in vanilla. That's what I do. Just mix it with milk.

Since I was a kid I like do patching. That's my bad habit. I used to make old coats, make it for long shorts for them, for the springtime. I used to patch up pants for kids just to keep myself busy. Lay coats out side by side, over with a thin cloth, both sides. To make a blanket.

Gee, I go through lots of hard times. Seems like I'm getting to know everything upside down.

I've been doing mechanic stuff, like that drawer. I try to fix my lamp; I can't do it. I find I can't fix things like that anymore.

I like to do carpenter work. More interesting. I had all the tools too. After I was married, the boys still get me some tools.

Nora on her eighty-sixth birthday. Mary Ann Bellis photo

My sons too. One day there's a big heavy parcel out there. For Mother's Day, hey. You know what it was? Electric drill.

I'm real poor housekeeper but I like to work on things. How can you keep the house clean when you're doing carpenter work? When you work on guitar, it takes all the time. I start think that way I feel quite all right. And who's going to do the cooking?

I always do crazy things... and I get away with it.

Thank you very much for listening.

Acknowledgements

Charlie Bellis initiated and guided this project. Maureen McNamara gave her vision, her joy and her dedicated work with Nora. *So You Girls Remember That* has been a collaboration. On behalf of Nora, Maureen, Charlie and myself, I thank the many people who offered their voice, support, patience and time over the years. Haw'aa. Thank you.

A special haw'aa to the late Naanii Mary Swanson for warm welcomes and patience, for transcriptions from poor quality cassette tapes, for translations, and for insights into the layers of meaning behind a word.

Thank you to the Bellis family for their support.

Haw'aa to all of the people who lent their voices to enrich the story, to Mary Ann Bellis, John Bellis, Danny Bellis, Frank Collison, Hazel Kirkwood and Margaret Adkins, and to those who have passed on: Claude Jones, Connie Webb, Leila Abrahams, Emma Matthews, Grace Wilson, Jean Schubert, Dick Bellis, Frieda Unsworth, Louisa Dixon, Henry Geddes, Adelia Dix, Betty and Albert Dalzell, Jessie Bradley, Claude Davidson, Mark Bell, Russell Samuels, Clarence Martin, Norman Stewart-Burton and Vicki Bragan.

This book was caught in a back eddy for years. Nika Collison volunteered to edit it. From "basically finished," it was confounding how many tweaks and rechecks and rewrites and such. Thank you, Nika. The book slumbered for two years more. Then Nora's great-granddaughter, Dana Bellis, bounced in, and it was suddenly happening. Dana's help was critical to getting it to the finish. And of course haw'aa to the eagle eyes of Pam Robertson, who worked with me on the final edit.

For generously sharing information, haw'aa to Andrew Bellis, the late Maddie Edgars, the late Robin and Rose Brown, Robin K. Wright, the late Cliff Armstrong and the Prince Rupert Anglican Church Synod Office, the Haida Language Nest Elders, Marianne Boelscher Ignace, Jaskwaan Bedard, Candace Weir, Lucille Bell, Vince Collison, John Broadhead, John Bennett, Rolly Williams and Kirk Thorgeirson.

I am grateful to the late Cindy Davies, Simon Davies, Marcia Crosby, Gwaai and Jaalen Edenshaw, Deirdre Brennan, Michelle Hollington, the late David Phillips, the late Dorothy and Emery Nelson, Sharon Matthews, Leslie Bellis, Sheila Cameron, Donna Edenshaw and more, for encouragement and feedback. I faced transcribing fifteen tapes by the start-and-stop tape recorder method. The next day Jack Litrell loaned me an old dictaphone. Thank you, Jack. And haw'aa to John Broadhead who kindly gifted the maps.

The Canada Council and the Bellis family provided financial support in 1992 for the initial transcribing.

Haw'aa to all those who shared photographs and expertise, especially Mary Ann Bellis, Dot Lewis and Jack Litrell.

I am most grateful for Nora's friendship. This is give back.

Contributors

CHARLIE BELLIS

Charlie Bellis was a hard-working man, a food gatherer and a commercial fisherman—Charlie and the *Lady Julia*.

Amongst other work he served on the Council of the Haida Nation and on the National Anglican Church Synod, and as a member of the mid-1980s Offshore Review Panel visited every village on the coast, and finally recommended that the moratorium on tanker traffic continue.

Charlie shared generously: food, skills and time, his friendship and his understandings. If a boat was in trouble at sea, Charlie's was the first boat heading out to help, even in a hurricane.

Charlie began the first Christmas Sail Past in 1984. Maybe two boats. No fireworks then. The *Lady Julia* all dressed up in Christmas lights. Past Masset to Old Massett and back, boats alight in the dark. The winter Sail Past is a yearly memorial to Charlie.

MAUREEN MCNAMARA

A Catholic and a Buddhist, Maureen had a huge belief in manifesting good, and so she lived.

Kick-ass parties, poetry and wine, a tea party with Elders, mossheads in the North Beach forest.

When a gold mine threatened the Yakoun River valley, Maureen became mother of the journal *Yakoun: River of Life*, from its first moments to finding exactly the right red for printing salmon drying on a rack.

Maureen lived life with joy and optimism and a devotion to the welfare of humanity. She and Naanii Nora manifested this oral history for us all.

JENNY NELSON

Jenny Nelson grew up in Fergus, Ontario, and has rooted on Haida Gwaii. Sometime teacher, sometime writer, mother, grandmother, she lives down by the harbour in Masset with dog Sal.

Endnotes

CHAPTER 1: SO YOU GIRLS REMEMBER THAT

1   Guudgas: "Guud means noise—the noise of chopping wood, packing gravel, whatever." Mary Swanson, personal communication, 2003. Linguistic note: Personal and place names are often shortened, but still represent the original name with its larger meanings.

2   Haida Gwaii was named the Queen Charlotte Islands from 1787 until 2010, when the English name was ceremonially returned to the province of BC in a bentwood box.

3   Nora's Recycling Tips: Tin cans with ends removed to hold rolled newspaper for fire-starter, holding-things toaster with a wire handle, plastic berry baskets with crocheted tops, all sorts of handles on all sorts of containers, lots and lots of crocheted wool bags, a small crocheted bag to hold bits of soap, a board with a wire handle and nails to hold spools of thread, a pin cushion full of Rose Spit sand. "When a needle are really rusty—look here [Nora runs a needle in and out of the sand bundle.] The sand is so fine."

4   My interpretation is that Nora's grandfather, Luke Bennett, risked becoming unlucky if he did not personally rebuild the fire when he came home. Naanii Mary Swanson suggested that it might have something to do with the opposite clan—that Luke, being an Eagle, ought not to warm himself with a home fire that his wife, a Raven, had built.

   "A person who wants to remain respected has to refrain from becoming unlucky and thus poor (iisanaa)." Marianne Boelscher, *The Curtain Within: Haida Social and Mythical Discourse* (Vancouver: UBC Press, 1988), p. 71.

5   Naa ḵajuud: John Enrico, "Draft on Names," unpublished manuscript, Old Massett, 1991, p. 9.

6   Gudaa x̱iigans: "One whose thought makes a noise," a female name of Yahgu 'laanaas lineage. John Enrico, "Draft on Names," p. 17.

7   The original clan was from Juus ḵaahlii. Luke Bennett is described as "a Tcets (Tsiij) Town Eagle… from Yan" in George F. MacDonald's *Haida Monumental Art: Villages of the Queen Charlotte Islands* (Vancouver: UBC Press, 1983), p. 148.

8   Kwii Gandlaas: Connie Webb, Prince Rupert, personal communica-
    tion, February 10, 1993. It was a Haida village on the west coast of Long
    Island, Alaska.

9   "When the Yakulanas give a feast they use Percy Brown right after Adam Bell
    [for the order of speakers]. In this case, Adam is recognized as head of the
    Masset Yakulanas. Percy Brown, who was senior male member of the Alaskan
    Haida group absorbed by the Masset Yakulanas, ranked second in this lineage."
    Mary Lee Stearns, *Haida Culture in Custody: The Masset Band* (Vancouver:
    Douglas & McIntyre, 1981), p. 225.

10 Other birthdates for Susan are given as 1857, about 1878 (Jan L. Fisher)
    and 1893.

11 The spelling of Kliijuuklaas is uncertain; it is probably Tlajuutl'aas. Source:
    Claude Jones.

12 English translations of the names are from Enrico, "Draft on Names," pp. 16–18.
         The initial translation I had for Kwah i'waans was Big bum. It turns out
    that this was wordplay, a friendly pun on his given name. "Some names lend
    themselves to puns, and Haidas love puns, using them jokingly in a familiar
    setting to make '…(low) names out of high names'. Done publicly, this could
    of course be taken as a serious insult…. Kwaa 7iiwans, officially 'the big blow-
    ing of the killer whale', becomes secularized to 'big rear-end' through a slight
    alteration in pronunciation." Boelscher, *The Curtain Within: Haida Social and
    Mythical Discourse*, p. 165.

13 "He is credited by Barbeau with holding the last pole-raising in Masset, when
    he raised a memorial in front of his house near the beach (22M2) during the
    1890's." MacDonald, *Haida Monumental Art*, p. 148. In 1969, Robert Davidson
    raised the Bear Mother pole in Massett.

14 Duuan 'iljuus: The name is recorded as a Tuuhlkk'a git'anee name, Git'ans sub-
    group 3, in Enrico, "Draft on Names," p. 9.

15 Sample records of Andrew Brown's birthdates:
         Nora: "He was about fifteen years old when the first missionary came,"
              i.e., born circa 1861.
         Marius Barbeau, *Haida Carvers in Argillite*, p. 203: "Born in 1865."
         Marriage record: 1870.
         Leslie Drew and Douglas Wilson, *Argillite: Art of the Haida*, p. 288: "1879."
         Charlie Bellis, personal communication: "Naanii Brown was his second
              wife and she was a girl when Andrew was first married."

16 Xahl gunjuus: Enrico, "Draft on Names," p. 10. Linguistic note: Xuhl or
    Xahl gunjuus.

17 Sdahl k'awaas was described as the Tsiits Git'ans wife of Kingaagwaaw
    by anthropologist George Peter Murdock in 1936. Murdock, whose main

consultant in Massett was their son, Captain Andrew Brown, provided a detailed account of Kingaagwaaw's and Sdahl k̲'aawaas's 'Waahlaal, or house-building potlatch, to convey yah G̲id, or high-rank status, on their children. Murdock, *Rank and Potlatch Among the Haida*, Yale University Publications in Anthropology Number 13, 1936; reprinted by Human Relations Area Files Press, New Haven, 1970. The name is spelled "StehlthKouwas" in the St. John's Church Missionary Society Marriage Record #42, 1887, Diocese of Caledonia, Prince Rupert, BC.

Murdock also noted that Kingaagwaaw's father St'aasd was the last surviving chief of the Duu Git'ans, a clan from the west coast of Graham Island closely related to the Tsiits Git'ans, who were the owners of the village G̲at'anaas ("Bilge-water-town") on Nasduu, or Hippa Island, and also owned houses at Tiiaan and subsequently at Yaakw.

Walter Kingaagwaaw was one of John R. Swanton's main storyteller consultants, and provided thirty-nine of the narratives in the collection of Masset Texts (1908). In addition, Swanton credits him with providing a large part of the information about northern Haida villages, village chiefs, lineage (clan) names, houses and house names in *Contributions to the Ethnology of the Haida* (1905).

Adam Bell, 'Laanaas sdang, also remembered Captain Andrew Brown as one of the last descendants of the Duu Git'ans who told several of the stories his father had dictated to Swanton to Adam, who then recorded them with Marianne Boelscher Ignace and his son, Lawrence Bell (Marianne Boelscher Ignace, personal communication).

18   "He was described by Alfred Adams, his contemporary, as a Gyitens [Git'ans] Eagle of Yan village and a member of the Stihltae family on his mother's side. The following information on Chief Stihltae was recorded by Dr. Swanton (The Haida... Jesup, p. 292): 'In Yan village, there was among many others, the 'House-looking-at- its-beak,' of which Steeltae—Returned—was the owner. The curved block of wood, which in the old times took the place of the house-pole on this house, bore the beak of a bird standing out in front.'" Barbeau, *Haida Carvers in Argillite*, pp. 204–205.

19   Kingaagwaaw: "News not wanted." Swanton translated his name as "he who does not wish the news of what he does spread abroad." Swanton, *Contributions to the Ethnology of the Haida*, p. 292. Enrico's "Draft on Names," p. 18, lists Kingee gwaa.u as a man's name under raww stl'angng 'lanngee (G̲aw Stl'ang 'laanaas), a sub-group of the stl'angng 'laanaas. Marius Barbeau recorded it as meaning "Hiding-his-own-fame." Barbeau, *Haida Carvers in Argillite*, p. 178.

20   "These brothers, members of the *Stlenga-lahnos*, sub-clan of the Eagles of Rosespit and Massett, were of modest extraction. *Stlenga-lahnos*, according

to Dr. Swanton, means 'People who dwell in the back part of the village.'" Barbeau, *Haida Carvers in Argillite*, pp. 178–79.

21   St. John's Church Missionary Society Marriage Record #42, 1887, Diocese of Caledonia, Prince Rupert, BC.

22   "The name of Gwaytihl, recorded by Dr. Swanton (Jesup..., p. 271), is K.'wai'ehl [K'waayeehl]; it means 'He-became-the-Eldest'... Gwaytihl died in 1912 (according to Alfred Adams). He was a good ninety. Rheumatism affected his hands in his old age. He used to fast in the old way; he would not drink or eat for forty days." Barbeau, *Haida Carvers in Argillite*, pp. 178–79.

   Robin K. Wright points out errors in Barbeau's text. She also notes that Prince Rupert marriage records show a second marriage indicating that the brothers Kingaagwaaw and Gwaay t'iihld were stepbrothers. Robin K. Wright, *Northern Haida Master Carvers*, p. 305.

23   Alfred Adams's sisters told Barbeau that John Gwaay t'iihld and a man named Nis.go carved all the poles at Yan, and that he also carved model houses. There are photographs of his work and a photo, assumed to be John, with a model house. Wright, *Northern Haida Master Carvers*, pp. 305, 308–11.

24   A photo of the tombstone can be seen in Wright, *Northern Haida Master Carvers*, p. 235.

25   Yaahl naaw: Yelthnou, from St. John's Church Missionary Society marriage record #42, Diocese of Caledonia, Prince Rupert, BC. Swanton lists Yaahl naaw of the Gaw Stl'ang 'laanaas as the owner of house No. 11 at Yan, noting that it is a Tlingit name and means "dead raven." Swanton, *Contributions of the Ethnology of the Haida*, p. 293.

26   Barbeau, *Haida Carvers in Argillite*, p. 178. Barbeau writes in more detail in his notes: "King-ego, Haida Carver," Marius Barbeau, National Museum, Ottawa, B.F.s50.12, pp. 1–3, in the Canadian Museum of Civilization Library.

   "Of King-ego and his brother Gwaytihl, sculptors and fellow craftsmen of Masset, on the Queen Charlotte Islands near the Alaskan border, we have identified a number of statuettes and high reliefs. Some of these carvings rank among the very best in the native art of the north West Coast.

   "King-ego,... whose original birth-place was Bear-Town, was a sculptor of argillite or black slate statuettes representing medicine men, chiefs in regalia, warriors, and odd types from among his people. His illustrations of the 'Bear Mother' myth are unsurpassed. And his small full-sized portrait of an Indian woman dressed as a white woman, exhibited at the Museum of Modern Art in New York, two years ago, was called a masterpiece (his identity then not being known). He is credited with a lot of large totem poles....

   "The statuettes and groups which these two brothers carved for white buyers differed on the whole from those of their fellow-craftsman insofar as the others preferred carving crests, emblems and totem poles, whereas they found inspiration in the ceremonial and daily life of their own tribe. Yet their realistic approach to art was not less stylistic than that of other Haidas of the same period.

"The medicine-men and sorcerers came first in King-ego's preferences, and the chiefs in regalia second. Almost every large museum in America holds recognizable specimens of this type from his hands. These figures were meant to be realistic, portrait-like in miniature. The features and expression appear authentic. They are typical West Coast personalities.

"The aims and efforts of the medicine-men as depicted of King-ego may be observed in his most ambitious work now preserved at the National Museum of Canada—a high relief showing medicine-men, their spirit helpers (Eagles and Frogs), and their patient, whose eyes are closed in agony. The leader of these mystic professionals holds in his left hand a magical crystal, and in his upraised left, a round rattle; and he is singing, his open mouth being pulled to one side. Through the septum of his nose runs a bone peg, symbol of his high rank.

"Nowhere else, even in Edenshaw's work, is the expression and plastic quality on the faces of this important group better achieved. Here are human pathos and suffering plainly revealed with a blend of realism and stylization that is seldom excelled anywhere. This other masterpiece stands at the forefront of Haida and North Pacific art.

"King-ego's considerable set of plastic portraits of chiefs in regalia, men and women, is much smaller than that of his medicine man, who were his preferences. His chiefs wear headdresses with crests and emblems, Chilkat or painted leather blankets, dance aprons with fringes, twisted cedar-bark collars of the secret society type, and occasionally they hold rattles in their hands.

"His illustrations of the 'Bear Mother' mythical tale are not a few; and they are outstanding. We find them in the Dawson Collection of McGill University, at the National Museum of Canada, and at the leading American museum for the Indians.... Nowhere, either in Asia or in North America, has a native artist bestowed as good a plastic quality upon this story as King-ego has repeatedly done in his later days, about 1900."

27   Barbeau, *Haida Carvers in Argillite*, p. 204.

CHAPTER 2: MASSETT

28   "Information from Alfred Adams," Northwest Coast Files, Marius Barbeau Collection, Canadian Museum of History, B-F-253.2.

29   Newton H. Chittenden, 1884, quoted in *Exploration of the Queen Charlotte Islands* (Vancouver: Gordon Soules, 1984), p. 70.

30　George A. Dorsey, "A Cruise Among Haida and Tlingit Villages about Dixon's Entrance," in Charles Lillard, *The Ghostland People: A Documentary History of the Queen Charlotte Islands, 1859–1906* (Victoria: Sono Nis Press, 1989), p. 285. Originally published in *Appletons' Popular Science Monthly*, Volume 53 (June 1898), from a lecture at Field Columbian Museum, November 6, 1897.

George Dorsey was known for his carelessness when hunting artifacts. In the 1890s, Charles Newcombe and Dorsey, with James Deans as their guide, visited Haida Gwaii. After one of these visits, Massett missionary James Henry Keen saw scattered hair and coffins. He was angry that the men had dug up graves for skulls and bones and didn't restore the gravesites. He complained by letter to the *Daily Colonist*. Dorsey recommended ignoring the complaint. For details on Dorsey's grave robberies in Haida Gwaii see Douglas Cole, *Captured Heritage: The Scramble for Northwest Coast Artifacts* (Vancouver: UBC Press, 1985) and also the documentary film *Stolen Spirits of Haida Gwaii* by Kevin McMahon.

31　The Hudson's Bay Company opened in Massett in 1870, temporarily run by Mr. A. Cooper, until postmaster M.H. Offutt, with labourer George McKay, could take over in 1874. "The returns at Masset consisted chiefly of fish oil, fur seals and sea otters." See Unknown, "Hudson's Bay Company Post At Masset Queen Charlotte Islands, 1869–1898," in *The Charlottes: A Journal of the Queen Charlotte Islands, Volume 2* (Skidegate: Queen Charlotte Islands Museum Society, 1973), p. 38.

According to Kathleen Dalzell, Massett's first trading post was originally built by an American, at a time when most villagers were away. When the Chiefs returned and found him trading liquor, villagers armed themselves and surrounded the building to evict him. "But after the first shot Charlie fled via a secret entrance and under cover of night made his way to the beach." He then walked the 100 miles to Skidegate and from there travelled by canoe to the mainland, where he offered the building and stock to the Hudson's Bay Company. The company had difficulty finding someone who would accept the post and be accepted by Massett people. Of Martin Offut, it is said that his "biggest asset was his Tsimpshean wife who was well-known and liked among the Haida. *Only* if she accompanied him would they permit the reopening of the post." Kathleen E. Dalzell, *The Queen Charlotte Islands, 1774–1966*, pp. 75–76. The post was closed June 1, 1898.

32　In 1862 the worst smallpox epidemic struck. The population of Massett fell from roughly 2,500 in 1835 (160 houses) to a few hundred by the 1870s. Measles, influenza and tuberculosis continued to take a toll well into the next century. I recommend *The Victoria Smallpox Crisis of 1862* by Grant Keddie, Royal British

Columbia Museum, published in *Discovery: Friends of the Royal British Columbia Museum Quarterly Review*, Volume 21, Number 4 (Autumn 1993).

33   This list of main villages is probably incomplete. There were many smaller villages and fish camps. Some people lived in Yan and Ḵang until a later date. Charlie Bellis heard that quite a few families lived at Yan. One family had two big dogs used for bear hunting and as pets. They would come over in their canoe to visit Massett. The dogs had muzzles of spruce roots. They never let the dogs aboard the canoe; they swam across. Charlie Bellis, personal communication, October 13, 1992.

Chief Edenshaw moved from Ya.aats to Massett in 1883. The last villages to be abandoned at the north end of Haida Gwaii were Yan and Ḵ'aayang in 1884. Massett then had twelve chiefs, with reduced families, with the resulting fragmentation of leadership and loyalties.

"Without question, the smallpox epidemic was the most important factor in the decline of Haida control over their territory. Yet the rapid decrease in population was critical not so much for its military implications as its effect on the Haida social and political system." Andrew Bellis, "The Masset Band," unpublished paper, History 353, Dr. Hendrickson, University of Victoria, April 16, 1992. p. 7.

34   W.H. Collison described Haida canoes as "the finest canoes in the world." "A whole fleet of new canoes are brought over annually, and sold to the mainland Indians, one proviso demanded in the payment being an old canoe or derelict, in which to make the return voyage to the Islands. Having obtained the old canoes, they set themselves to repair and strengthen them, and then, filling them with cargoes of fish grease and other provisions, they make the return journey by coasting along the southeastern shores of Alaska until Cape Muzon or Chacon is reached. Here they encamp, and await a favorable opportunity to sail across to the north of the Queen Charlotte Islands." William H. Collison, *In the Wake of the War Canoe*, p. 110.

Collison also notes: "It is to be regretted that no provision has been made to preserve a sufficient supply of the best red cedar to enable the Haida to continue their canoe building. In a few years this industry will have passed away and one of the most interesting features of Indian life will have been forgotten." Collison, *In the Wake of the War Canoe*, p. 168.

35   In 1861, one of the Colony of Vancouver Island's first legislative acts denied Indigenous people the right to pre-empt land—pre-emption being the process by which settlers could own land. With proof of residency, improvements and a survey, land could be purchased at a discount or without charge.

In 1866, the Colonies of Vancouver Island, British Columbia and Queen Charlotte Islands became the united Colony of British Columbia, with Victoria as its capital. One of its first acts, a Colonial Land Ordinance, reconfirmed pre-emptions of 160–320 acres, "provided that it did not go to Aborigines of this Continent." Land Ordinance, 1970, R.S.B.C. 1871, c. 144, Section 3, from "Federal and Provincial Legislation Restricting and Denying Indian Rights," p. 4, in Joe Mathias and Gary R. Yabsley, *Conspiracy of Legislation: The Suppression of Indian Rights in Canada*, report, January 21, 1986. Reprinted in *BC Studies* Number 89 (Spring 1991).

In 1882, Peter O'Reilly, Indian Reserve Commissioner, came to mark the first Haida reserves. "'In Massett I commenced my work, having had an interview with the principal chief, 'Wee-ah', and a few of his people, the greater portion of the tribe being absent engaged in fishing. I fully explained the object of my mission and the desire of the Dominion Government to see his people advance in civilization and living more like their white brethren, to which he replied that they had long expected me, and were glad that at last their lands were to be secured for them.'" O'Reilly to Superintendent General of Indian Affairs, October 24, 1882, RC10, Records of Indian Reserve Commission, Letter book (1882–1884), V1275, Mf. B-1391, BCARS. See also Charles Lillard, *Just East of Sundown: The Queen Charlotte Islands* (Victoria: TouchWood Editions, 1995), pp. 114–15.

Sixteen reserves were recorded, totalling 1,871.5 acres (about five acres a person), with loss of much of their natural resource base.

"Clearly, the implications of their loss was not readily apparent to the Masset Haida in 1882." Nora's grandson Andrew Bellis, "The Masset Band," unpublished paper, History 353, Dr. Hendrickson, University of Victoria, April 16, 1992, p. 9.

36 For other suggested birthdates for Susan Brown, see Chapter 1, endnote 10, and for Andrew Brown, Chapter 1, endnote 15.

37 Emily was the first white child born on Haida Gwaii.

38 From records of "Baptisms at St. John's Church, Massett," and the "Birth/Death" records, the Anglican Church Synod Office, Prince Rupert, with Haida names added.

The children of Andrew and Susan Brown (names of those who baptized them in parentheses):

Eliza, G̱uuhlaaljaad (Green [copper] paint woman), born August 1891, baptized September 27, at one month, died June 1978 (J.H. Keen)

Madden, baptized December 31, 1893, at four months, died

Jessie, baptized December 23, 1894, at three weeks, died

Johnson, baptized December 27, 1896, at ten weeks, died (J.H. Keen)

Polly, Ilsgidee (Great), baptized April 10, 1898

Johnson, born December 3, 1899, baptized December 24, died ca. 1905
(W.E. Collison)

Robert, born November 1900, baptized February 10, 1901, died ca. 1906
(W.E. Collison)

Nora, Gaadgas, born October 10, 1902, baptized December 28, died May 6,
1997 (W.E. Collison)

Heber, born October 28, 1904, baptized November 20

Archie, Skil ḵiiyaas (Light wealth spirit), born 1905, died April 20, 1932

Percy Patrick, Tlajaang, born January 26, 1906, baptized November 6,
died 1979 (W.E. Collison)

John, born May 4, 1908, baptized June 8, death date unknown (W.E.
Collison)

Oley (Ole), born June 2, 1910, baptized September 4, died May 29, 1939
(Wm. Hogan)

Fritz Chapman, born December 6, 1913, baptized February 8, 1914, died
August 10, 1934 (H.H. Greene)

Gideon, born August 28, 1915, baptized December 5, died May 25, 1926
(J.M. Crarey)

Ezra, born October 6, 1917, baptized January 20, 1918, died March 7, 1930
(Alfred E. Price)

Notes:

Although there is a record of Heber's birth, I don't recall Nora referring to a
brother Heber.

Archie's Haida name and birthdate come from informants and from
Enrico, "Draft on Names," Family Tree #25.

Percy "was born January 26, 1906, at his mother's home at Kake, Prince
of Wales Island, Alaska… Percy died in March of this year [1979]." Margaret B.
Blackman, *Tales from the Queen Charlotte Islands, Book 1* (Masset: Regional
Council, Senior Citizens of the Queen Charlotte Islands, 1979), p. 54.

Captain Andrew Brown was baptized in 1933, son of "Walter & Elizabeth
Brown, adult, Fisherman." He was buried January 18, 1962.

Two children, Madden and Jessie, were born to Andrew and *Sarah* Brown
in 1893 and 1894. According to research by Jan L. Fisher, Susan Brown used
the name Sarah in church records prior to 1895. She was baptized March 31,
1895, as Susan Brown. Also from Jan Fisher's research come the death dates of
Archie, Percy, Ole, Fritz, Gideon and Ezra.

CHAPTER 3: JACOB'S LADDER

39 Skil ḵiiyaas. I have not been able to track this person in any records. Charlie Bellis said that the man fell overboard, past the bar, and that there were hard feelings between the families for many years afterward.

40 Fate of the dead: "Not all of the dead went to the Land of Souls. Those who were drowned went to live with the killer-whales. According to one man, they went to the house of The-One-in-the-Sea first, where they had their fins fitted on, after which they went round into the houses of the other killers. When killer-whales appeared in front of a town, it was thought that they were human beings who had been drowned and took this way to inform the people. These persons thus became supernatural beings." John R. Swanton, *Contributions of the Ethnology of the Haida*, Memoirs of the American Museum of Natural History, Volume VIII. Reprint from V, Part I, of the Jesup North Pacific Expedition. Franz Boas, ed. Leiden: E.J. Brill / New York: G.E. Stechert, 1905, pp. 35–36.

41 Connie Webb, personal communication, Prince Rupert, February 10, 1993. It was customary for personal possessions to be laid out with the body. The red and blue beads may have been glass trade beads.

42 Claude Jones, in personal communication, said Robert Bennett was given the name Yaahldaats'ee when he took a lot on the hill at Iits'aaw. He inherited the house and name from his uncle.

43 Smiijuu means cute little child. John Enrico, *Haida Dictionary: Skidegate, Masset and Alaskan Dialects, Volume 1* (Fairbanks: Alaska Native Language Center, University of Alaska / Juneau: Sealaska Heritage Institute, 2005), p. 393.

44 "He's the one [Andrew Brown] don't like to lay around. He was carving a doll for one of us. Soon's the doll's face come out of the red cedar, the girl just hug it. Wouldn't let him touch it again." Connie Webb, personal communication, 1993.

45 "Children's activities seemed to be generally segregated by sex in Florence's time, as she noted that 'boys played together and girls played together.'" Margaret B. Blackman, *During My Time: Florence Edenshaw Davidson, A Haida Woman* (Seattle: University of Washington Press / Vancouver: Douglas & McIntyre, 1982), p. 27.

"Nora never used to like to play with dolls. She'd rather have a hammer or an axe or something. She still do." Connie Webb, personal communication, 1993.

Nora wasn't the only tomboy. Connie Webb: "I remember Mom used to make bloomers, so I wouldn't wear a dress. I had nothing but boys—Oley, Fritz, Gideon, and... Edgar and Peter Jones and Edwin Jones. They were all boys... run to north beach to catch a wild horse. Edwin would get on and they throw me on too. That's why Mom made bloomers."

46 Nora: "I think it was big canoes. I don't remember. Those big canoes I guess. So many of them on it my mother used to say. They just tell me about it. I don't remember. I didn't even know I was the leader for the boys. They just keep talking about it."

47 Tattooing with lineage crests was part of a coming of age ceremony, marked by a potlatch. Nora's parents and uncles had tattoos. Claude Jones said that Susan's brothers were "the last ones in the village to have tattoos." An uncle potlatched for the boys when they were tattooed.

"Brown had the Eagle tattooed on his right leg, and his brothers, so he said, had theirs on their chests. The four special crests of his clan were—the Eagle, *Tseeda*; the Skate, *Hlkyan-kwestan*; the Frog; and *Tsen*, the Incisors of the Beaver." Barbeau, *Haida Carvers in Argillite*, p. 204.

48 "Informant Captain Andrew Brown," Canadian Museum of Civilization Library, Archives and Documentation, Marius Barbeau Collection, Northwest Coast Files, Folder: "Haida Totems in General" (B.F. 285). B.B. 285.64.

49 Nora's cousin Connie Webb said that Nora "was sickly when she was young. Her mom never used to let her do anything."

50 "Big-Eagle (*Owt'-iwans* [G̱uud i'waans]) became his Haida name as a chief, after it had been given up by his (maternal) grandfather, who had been chief of Nisto (or Hippah) Island on the northwestern side of the Queen Charlotte group." Barbeau, *Haida Carvers in Argillite*, p. 204.

Barbeau was occasionally wrong on details of kinship. There is no record of Andrew Brown's maternal grandfather being chief at Nasduu (Hippa Island). However, his paternal grandfather Charles St'aasd is on record as the last Duu Git'ans chief of G̱at'anaas ("Bilge-water-town" on Nasduu), the Duu Git'ans being closely related to the Tsiits Git'ans, Andrew Brown's clan. See Murdock, *Rank and Potlatch Among the Haida*, pp. 11–12. Adam Bell also remembered that Andrew Brown had the name G̱uud i'waans from his "father's father's side" at Nasduu (Hippa Island). Nora points out that Andrew Brown's nephew Andrew Yorke's inherited the name G̱ud i'waans through his maternal clan, not through his father's side.

51 Florence Davidson, Jaad ahl ḵ'iiganaa, meaning Story maid or Woman about whom myths are told. Florence was married on February 23, 1911. Her father was carver Charles Edenshaw.

52 According to Nora, Bob Johnson built the house, later Alec Taylor's house, at the end of Wilson Street, New Masset.

53 Charlie Bellis, February 1993: "Then, they [the grandparents] were still going out fishing but not doing well. Teddy went out with them on the *Ruth G*. They parked it in front of David's [David Phillips's]. Someone bought it. It was fishing out of Nanaimo for years. The thing ran until just a couple years ago."

54 Percy Brown, "Percy Brown," in "Northern Haida Land and Resource Utilization: A Preliminary Overview," in Margaret B. Blackman, *Tales from the Queen Charlotte Islands: Book 2* (Masset: Senior Citizens of the Queen Charlotte Islands), p. 54.

55 Barbeau, *Haida Carvers in Argillite*, pp. 204–205.

56 "It was from his father Kingego, the sculptor of statuettes of Slinglanaws (Rear-Town), that Andrew Brown learned carving. 'He is ever ready to put out his work, and he does not consider it inferior to the best,' according to Peter Hill of Massett. 'Of whatever quality his work, he always boasts 'That's fine!' He is a great joker and is known in Massett, his native town, as a good entertainer. He tells many tales and can make up a good story. Without a school education, he is a pretty smart old boy. During the summers, he fishes and seines salmon, having a large seine boat, even now, in his old age. And, in the slack winter months, he does his slate work.'" Barbeau, *Haida Carvers in Argillite*, pp. 203–206.

57 Leslie Drew and Douglas Wilson, *Argillite: Art of the Haida*, p. 113.

58 Tliiyaa: I'm uncertain if this is the right word. Tliiyaa may refer to a dance that was part of the winter activity in Massett in the 1890s.

"Wintertime when I was small they used to dance so much… They just did it for the fun so they don't forget them…. I remember when they used to dance 'kliya'…. They used to go around the village saying, 'We're going to see 'kliya' tonight,' and all the children would be real excited. The mask was real big and wide with a big nose and mouth. The eyes were red and behind the mouth was red. Little kids used to be really scared of it." Florence Davidson, in Blackman, *During My Time*, p. 84.

There is a Haida mask in Pitt River Museum, Oxford, England, possibly collected by Charles Harrison. Live coals could be placed behind large red fabric eyes to make the eyes glow red.

Jaalen Edenshaw was told by Nora's cousin, Adelia Dix, that this mask was danced before the main performance, the first dancer out. She was the lady who would come and get naughty children.

CHAPTER 4: I REMEMBER A LITTLE BIT

59 Naanii Emma Matthews, cassette recording of Yakoun River Elders, 1988.

60 Naanii Emma Matthews, personal communication, February 23, 1989.

61 Mark Bell, personal communication, July 18, 1989.

62 The suffix "gung" is added to a name, meaning "father of," for instance, Charliegung—Charlie's father.

63 Yan is still sometimes called "The Gardens." Sitka black-tailed deer were first introduced to the Islands by Reverend W.E. Collison, circa 1878, and again by

the province of BC in 1911, 1912, 1913 and 1925. Deer predation destroyed crops for Haidas and settlers alike.

64 Grace Wilson, recorded by Maureen McNamara (undated).

65 "Gligu, according to Percy Brown, refers to 'something with a nice point on it.' The term is most frequently used to refer to the digging stick used to collect clams, chitons, edible roots, and spruce roots. Though a gligu might be used by anyone, it was thought of primarily as a woman's tool, and was symbolic of women's economic activities. Percy Brown noted, 'at marriage every woman's got to have a gligu and every man a fishing line.'" Margaret B. Blackman, "Notes," in *Tales from the Queen Charlotte Islands*, p. 52.

66 Rolly Williams recalls Naanii Florence Davidson talking about rowing. Some boats had two sets of oars, and there would be a steersman in the stern to steer with a paddle.

67 The Haida potato: "The current Haida potato... [was] returned to the Islands by Victor Adams and was grown after an absence of fifty years. Were it not for Emily Thompson taking seed stock to Ketchikan fifty years ago and successive generations of these potatoes cultivated perhaps this living link with a distinct culture would have disappeared." David Phillips, in *Growing Food on the Queen Charlotte Islands*, eds. Jane Kinegal and Sam Simpson (Masset: Friends of the Library, 1986), p. 88.

68 "Until 1923 Indians were not allowed to operate engine-powered boats in the north coast commercial fishery." In 1923, Indigenous People were given the right "to hold commercial ocean-fishing licences." Paul Tennant, *Aboriginal Peoples and Politics* (Vancouver: UBC Press, 1990), pp. 73, 103.

69 Transcription and translation, Mary Swanson.

70 Nora was visiting the T'aalan Stl'ang Rediscovery Camp on the northwest coast of Graham Island, Haida Gwaii, which was at that time led by Huckleberry (Thom Henley). On a small offshore island in the bay lies the Lepas Bay Ecological Reserve, which protects Leach's storm petrels.

71 According to Mary Swanson, "Ḵiid" means spruce or evergreen tree. Here Nora refers to the Golden Spruce, which grew in Juskatla on the west bank of the Yakoun River. It was disrespectfully cut down in 1997. The Haida led the island community in a memorial service on the riverbank. See Caroline Abrahams, "Ḵiid Ḵiiyaas," a story of the Golden Spruce, in *Yakoun: River of Life* (Massett: Council of the Haida Nation, 1990).

72 People often ate from a bowl in the middle of the table. Each person would have a large, deep wooden or horn spoon, which served as both bowl and spoon. Nora once told me about the time she lost the spoons. She was young. Her family was camping across the inlet, up the inlet a little way, by a creek.

She was down at the creek washing the spoons. The call came that they were leaving so she ran to the boat and left all the spoons behind by the creek.

73   Bear Song translation, Mary Swanson. Also may be found in: John Enrico and Wendy Bross Stuart, *Northern Haida Songs*, pp. 91–92.

74   SG̱aanaa means "be a spirit." SG̱aanuwaa means "big animal" and "be supernatural." Linguistic note: In Massett dialect the sound written as G̱ usually sounds similar to a glottal stop. In Skidegate dialect it is pronounced like a *g* that is far down in the throat.

75   Nora taught the Bear Song to Claude and Sarah Davidson's dance group. She was to sing the song, so she came dressed like a young boy. Instead, she was asked to play the role of the grandmother and still sing the song. Hence Nora was uncomfortable because it was the boy's song. As Nora described it: "And that was him that start to. That song got in his mind. Not his grandmother. I could be dressed for it. You know that hunting song. It's supposed to be a little boy. And I could have a fur around, had panty hose underneath it, and a hat on with a feather on and something around. Just like a little boy."

76   Willie Matthews, Jimmy Harris and John Geddes were tried at Old Massett on April 6, 1935, by Stipendiary Magistrate A.R. Mallory.

The judgement reads: "It was found that the above were fishing in the area described under the Section of the Regulations under which the charge was laid conflicts with Acts regulating the rights of Indians to fish for food and that in Regulations and Acts governing Indians where the word person or persons occur it does not refer to Indians.

"Therefor[e] this Court has decided that it has no Authority, Power or Jurisdiction to impose penalty on the above named Indians for fishing for food in the area described."

77   Charlie Bellis, personal communication, February 3, 1993. Charlie draws from Thomas Berger's address to the Canadian Ethnology Society, "Native Rights in the New World: A Glance at History," in Banff, Alberta, February 24, 1979, p. 3. Berger refers to the Catholic bishop Bartholomé de Las Casas, bishop of Chiapas, Mexico, in the sixteenth century. In 1550, in Valladolid, Spain, Las Casas publicly debated with a leading philosopher who argued Aristotle's pro-slavery doctrine of superior and inferior peoples. In Berger's words, "Las Casas, on the other hand, argued that all men are endowed with natural rights, that the Europeans had no right to enslave the Indians, that the peoples of the Americas had a right to live" as free men. While Spanish expeditions to the new world were "suspended," the two men debated before a junta of fifteen "theologians, judges and court officials." In the end, the junta made no decision.

78 Ḵawk'ahl is the word for "to save food to take home," as is done at feasts and potlatches. Jordan Lachler, *Dictionary of Alaskan Haida* (Juneau: Sealaska Heritage Institute, 2010), p. 238.

CHAPTER 5: THEY USED TO EXPLAIN TO US WHAT'S THE MEANING OF IT

79 From Dadens, "Middle Town."

80 Transcription and translation: Mary Swanson and Marianne Boelscher Ignace.

81 I compiled this story from six separate tellings. The lines noted with a [†] are from a similar version except that Butterfly is replaced by Eagle. Referring to stories of the Raven cycle, Marianne Boelscher Ignace writes, "In some of them… Eagle appears as Stlaḵam, 'butterfly', who acts as Raven's 'servant' and 'companion', although this also accords him the role of 'spokesman', granting him implicit power." Later she notes that Raven "kills Butterfly, his companion, 'cousin' and servant, eats him, and makes him alive again." Boelscher, *The Curtain Within: Haida Social and Mythical Discourse*, pp. 32, 180.

82 Charlie Bellis, personal communication, February 3, 2003. As Paul Tennant notes, "For individual Indians survival was a matter of economics rather than politics.… The coastal fishing industry provided the major exception, becoming the only economic sector in the province in which prominent Indians were economically better off than most local Whites and in which the leading Indians were regarded by local Whites as their equals in ability and initiative.… The coastal commercial fishermen were an important force in the evolution of Indian political activity, especially during the period of political prohibition from 1927 to 1951." Tennant, *Aboriginal Peoples and Politics*, pp. 73–74.

83 The potlatch: gyaa 7isdla, "giving things away." Boelscher, *The Curtain Within*, p. 66. Lineages, or clans, formed the basis of Haida economy. From lineage resources, wealth was accumulated. A potlatch was a feast during which this wealth was given away. It was the ceremonial last step to raising and validating social and political status. The public was paid with gifts to act as witnesses, to acknowledge or refute. Canadian law made potlatches illegal from 1884 to 1951.

84 Saagaa: a particular war dance. See Number 28, "Possible Women's Battle Song," in Enrico and Stuart, *Northern Haida Songs*, p. 155. Elsewhere, Enrico and Stuart comment on this dance: "The Haida term for the war songs sung by warriors' wives is not given in any source. Swanton's translation was 'sk'aGaaw killed many'… The use of these songs is completely unknown. Swanton's account above also mentions dancing by the warriors' wives, led by the wife of the leader of the war party.… The singers would walk along in a line with the song leader dancing somewhat ahead and dodging from side to side. One man in the line of dancers held a lance without a point, which he aimed at the

leader at intervals. Finally, he would throw the lance at the leader, deliberately missing him, and would pick it up again and spear him. The leader would then groan out the phrase yaa laa laa sii and pretend to expire.... Consultants said the dance described here could include both men and women. It seemed to have been last performed in the 1940s." And: "Another possible source of the song is that it is of the Tlingit genre of 'funny songs' that were sung by the wives of the captors of a Deer (peace envoy) at a peace ceremony while their husbands danced with mock weapons." Enrico and Stuart, *Northern Haida Songs*, Song #91, pp. 41, 499 (notes).

85   Translation: Mary Swanson.

86   Doorway: an entrance hole in the base, or on either side, of a house frontal totem pole.

87   Big House: "Monster House," the largest longhouse on Haida Gwaii, built by Chief Wiiaa (Weah) circa 1840. It was a fifty-five-foot-square house. It was demolished about 1901. MacDonald, *Haida Monumental Art*, p. 142.

CHAPTER 6: BUT I WAS HAPPY AT HOME

88   Charles Sheldon, "The Elusive Caribou," in Charles Lillard, *The Ghostland People* (Victoria: Sono Nis Press, 1989), p. 296.

89   Thomas Deasy, Indian Agent, letter, 3 George V., A. 1913, p. 246, from Indian Affairs (RG10, Volume 1661) 29-200 159, p. 2.

90   "Bishop Du Vernet's Visit to the Queen Charlotte Islands," in *North British Columbia News*, Volume 2, Number 15 (July 1913), pp. 35–36.

91   Transcription: Mary Swanson.

92   Douglas Jones, "Douglas Jones Abroad, Chapter 11: A Visit to Old Massett." *North British Columbia News*, Volume IV, Number 17 (January 1914), p. 3.

93   Thomas Deasy to Prince Rupert, September 1911, p. 2.

94   Thomas Deasy, Indian Agent, Letter to Department of Indian Affairs, Ottawa, Ont., from Q.C. Agency, Massett Reserve, January 2, 1912, Thomas Deasy, pp. 2–5, #15-18, copy Feb.12.1912.

95   Department of Indian Affairs p. 396, 3 George V., A. 1913, Indian Affairs (RG 10, Volume 1661) 29-200, 159-160, pp. 3–4.

96   Indian Agent's Office p. 156, 222-200 L9 200, Indian Affairs (RG10, Volume 1661).

97   There were three Indian residential schools in Chilliwack, BC: the Presbyterian Coqualeetza Indian Residential School, 1861–1940, the Roman Catholic residential school, and the Methodist Coqualeetza School, 1896–1937. The Methodist school eventually became a TB quarantine hospital. There was an earlier industrial school much closer to Massett, at Metlakatla, but it was closed. Connie Webb: "I went to Coqualeetza, 1924–1928, when I was eleven years old. I hated it. Two hours a day school, the rest you work—wash the floor, scrub the floor.

It was at Sardis, three miles from Chilliwack. It burned, thank goodness." Old Massett and Skidegate tried for a decade, unsuccessfully, to get a school on the Islands.

98 "Perhaps worst of all, the schools were death traps. Because of overcrowding, inadequate diet and poor construction, the buildings were incubators of disease, chiefly tuberculosis. In 1907, the Indian department's medical inspector reported that an astonishing sixty-nine percent of residential students had died as a result of their school experience." KnowBC Blog, "Where Mountains Meet the Sea: A Coastal History," Chapter 3, Part 5: "The Residential Schools," KnowBC.com, June 27, 2010.

CHAPTER 7: SONG

99 Reverend F.P. Throman, "New Church At Massett Completed," *North British Columbia News* Number 44 (May 1921), p. 12. St. John the Evangelist Church was consecrated on May 7, 1887.

"By 1921 the church built in Harrison's time was too small for the 400 communicant members at Old Masset, and although there was a church at New Masset as well (St. Paul's, built in 1916), a larger building was undertaken. On 6 February 1921 the second St. John the Evangelist was formally opened by Archdeacon Collison." Hugh McCullum and Karmel Taylor McCullum, *Caledonia: One Hundred Years Ahead* (Toronto: Canada Anglican Book Centre, 1979), p. 54.

"They'd work on the church and go down to eat at the hall. Andrew Brown, he didn't work on the church, so he said at a dinner he'd buy the bell. It would be heard clear to Port Simpson. Under Florence's house. It cracked and they were going to fix it but didn't." Henry Geddes, personal communication, July 1989. The church was burned down by an arsonist in the 1970s.

100 Transcription: Mary Swanson. A more complete version of the song and background information may be found in Enrico and Stuart, *Northern Haida Songs*, Song #90A, sung by Florence Davidson, 1977, pp. 313–14. The composer was Neelans (Richard Neylants) ca. 1842–1923, p. 59. "Neelans composed this song when three men, David Jones, Elijah Jones, and William Matthews, graduated from Metlakatla school around 1910, David becoming organist, and the other two lay readers. Since these men had fathers in Neelans' lineage, they were 'sons' to the composer." p. 314.

101 Transcription and translation: Mary Swanson and Marianne Boelscher Ignace. The song may be found in Enrico and Stuart, *Northern Haida Songs*, Song #91, sung by Robert Davidson Sr. and Florence Davidson, 1969, pp. 317–19. Composer: Neelans.

102	Transcription and translation: Mary Swanson. Version of song in Enrico and Stuart, *Northern Haida Songs*, Song #95, sung by Emily Thompson, 1969, pp. 329–31. Composer: Skil rahlaas (George Harris), ca. 1866–90.

103	Transcription and translation: Mary Swanson.

104	Leslie Drew and Douglas Wilson, *Argillite: Art of the Haida* (North Vancouver: Hancock House, 1980), p. 29.

105	William H. Collison, *In the Wake of the War Canoe*, 1915, reprint, edited and annotated by Charles Lillard (Victoria: Sono Nis Press, 1981), p. 156. Dancing was also an important part of storytelling but was curtailed and moved into people's homes. Collison wrote: "Dancing, which was carried out every night without intermission during our first winter on the Islands, has been greatly checked." Letter from W.H. Collison, dated April 4, 1878, Church Missionary Society, London. In Leslie Drew and Douglas Wilson, *Argillite: Art of the Haida* (North Vancouver: Hancock House, 1980), p. 90.

106	Bishop of Caledonia, F.H. Du Vernet, "Bishop Du Vernet's Visit to the Queen Charlotte Islands," *North British Columbia News* Volume 2, Number 15 (July 1913), p. 36.

107	"Interesting Reminiscences of Henry Edenshaw," Mrs. V.A. de B. Davies, upon the death of Henry Edenshaw, *North British Columbia News*, an insert from the *Vancouver Province* (ca. 1935), p. 283.

CHAPTER 8: AND SO I LEFT MASSETT RIGHT TO HERE

108	From March 1918 to June 1920 there was a viral strain of subtype H1N1, an influenza pandemic particularly attacking young, healthy adults, which ultimately killed an estimated 50 million people worldwide. The huge troop movements of World War I helped to spread the disease.

109	Alice (1891–1958) and Lily were daughters of Martha Neilson (née Young). Nora refers to Alice's son, Lee Edenshaw. Lily was Wilfred Bennett's mother. Alice married Reuben (Jimmy) Harris. She later moved to Alaska with her children. Her son Lee remained in Massett, having been adopted by Henry Edenshaw. When his daughter married, Lee lived with Daisy and Geoffrey White. Robert Bennett adopted Wilfred. According to Nora: "Wilfred Bennett was adopted. He [Robert Bennett] adopt three kids altogether. He got a girl. She died, got a big family and she died. Dorcas her name was. And another boy from his own brother from Hydaberg. Somebody went and kicked him. Real cheeky boy and he gets a big man mad and he kick him around. He must have break his lungs or something. He didn't live too long."

110	Wallace Fisheries set up in 1910 in Naden Harbour. In 1919 it moved to the Watun River. Wallace Fisheries sold to BC Fishing and Packing Company in 1926. There was a village at Watun River from 1920 to 1930.

111   Jessie Bradley, personal communication (undated). Jessie grew up on a home-stead near Rose Spit.

CHAPTER 9: I NEVER CAME BACK HOME AGAIN

112   Miss D.M. Outram, "Notes From The Farthest West," *North British Columbia News*, ca. July 1911.

113   Ruth Turney, "The Mission Boats," in *Tales from the Queen Charlotte Islands, Book 2* (Masset: Regional Council, Senior Citizens of the Queen Charlotte Islands, 1982), p. 107.

114   "'Cooking'… signifies a common-law relationship. The term is used in this manner by older women who have been 'housekeepers' or 'cooked for' white men." Mary Lee Stearns, *Haida Culture in Custody: The Masset Band* (Vancouver: Douglas & McIntyre, 1981), p. 171.

115   James Gillette was the Anglican minister in Masset, from 1923 to 1926. In 1926 he gave up the ministry to become the Indian Agent.

116   Nora and Fred were married June 30, 1931.

117   Charlie Bellis was born in 1932.

118   Howard B. Phillips, "Fred Bellis—An Unforgettable Character," in *Tales from the Queen Charlotte Islands, Book 2* (Masset: Regional Council, Senior Citizens of the Queen Charlotte Islands, 1982), pp. 107–10. When the New Masset Community Hall was rebuilt, "Fred Bellis came up with a large round drum fur-nace." Howard B. Phillips, *The New Massett Community Club* (Tlell: Fingerprints, 1986), p. 13.

119   Alfred E. Price, "Good News from Massett," *Northern British Columbia News* Number 36 (May 1917), p. 55.

120   A naval wireless station was set up in 1942, a few miles north of New Masset, as a high-frequency direction finder intercept station and as a relay for ship-to-shore communications. It was able to locate the signal source almost instantly. Built in 1971 as part of a worldwide network, the last surviving stations are in Gander, Newfoundland, and in Masset.

       The Royal Canadian Air Force arrived in 1943 (staying until 1946). A steel mat landing strip was built on the beach off Minaker Road and a prefab camp set up. By 1944, there were sixty-odd servicemen stationed there.

       "During the war, Dad felt really bad when three Air Force boys sunk off Edenshaw. One or two of them drowned. Henry Geddis got the engine out of the boat." Charlie Bellis, personal communication.

121   Mrs. Robertson was Charlie's godmother. He described her as "strict as hell." She lived in a house across the street from Nora and Fred, in what is now Copper Beech House, at the corner of Delkatla Street and Collison Avenue,

Masset. She planted the array of flowering trees, an English garden, which people are still enjoying.

Hazel Kirkwood grew up on the Evans farm on Kumdis Island. She used to spend a week a year with Mrs. Robertson. She describes her as "a class-conscious English lady. She insisted on the very specifics when setting table. She used to urge the younger Bellis children to bath at her place weekly, on Saturdays." Personal communication, Dixon Entrance Maritime Museum, September 11, 2001.

122 Jean married Dudley James (Jim) Schubert in 1948. His father was Dudley Charles Schubert, superintendent of BC and Yukon Telegraphs until it was sold to BC Telephone. His great-grandmother, Catherine O'Hare Schubert, came from County Down, Ireland. She was the first white woman to cross the Canadian Rockies. She travelled in an ox cart, pregnant, with her two boys. She wouldn't let her husband go alone. The baby, Rose, was born in Kamloops. There is a monument to Catherine in Armstrong, BC.

123 Thomas Deasy, Indian Agent, letter, 3 George V., A., 1913, from Indian Affairs (RG10, Volume 1661) 29-200 159, p. 2.

124 Special Committees of the Senate and House of Commons to Inquire into the Claims of the Allied Tribes of British Columbia, *Proceedings, Reports and the Evidence* (Ottawa: King's Printer, 1927).

125 Paul Tennant, *Aboriginal Peoples and Politics* (Vancouver: UBC Press, 1990), pp. 111–12. Amendment to the Indian Act, Section 141: "Every person who, without the consents of the Superintendent General expressed in writing, receives, obtains, solicits or requests from any Indian any payment or contribution or promise of any payment or contribution for the purpose of raising a fund or providing money for the prosecution of any claim which the tribe or band of Indians to which such Indian belongs, or of which he is a member, has or is represented to have for the recovery of any claim or money for the benefit of the said tribe or band, shall be guilty of an offence and liable upon summary conviction for each such offence to a penalty not exceeding two hundred dollars and not less than fifty dollars or to imprisonment for any term not exceeding two months."

CHAPTER 10: AND I WAS LEFT ALONE WITH THE SIX CHILDREN

126 At this time, Nora lived in a house on Main Street, where the Northern Savings Credit Union is now, across from the old police station building. Her daughter, Jean Schubert, remembered, "The house burned to the ground. Mom only cried for her pictures."

127 Sam Simpson, "Adventures in the Crab Trade," *Tales from the Queen Charlotte Islands, Book 2* (Masset: Regional Council, Senior Citizens of the Queen Charlotte Islands, 1982), p. 95.

128 Sam Simpson, "Adventures in the Crab Trade," *Tales from the Queen Charlotte Islands, Book 2*, p. 88.

129 Andrew Yorke's father, John, died in a longshoring accident in Prince Rupert.

CHAPTER 11: WE SHOULD UNDERSTAND PROPER WAY

130 Russell Samuels, personal communication, January 25, 2002.

131 Marianne Boelscher Ignace: "What Leila and Nora are referring to here is the story about the Origin of Carved House-posts, in Swanton Masset Texts #30, told by Walter Kingaagwaaw, who must have told this story to Andrew Brown, who then told it to Leila and Nora."

132 "A Skidegate man who had been much among the whites said that his people used to pray to Power-of-the-Shining-Heavens 'just as white people pray to God.'... Nor do I think that we have the effects of missionary teaching here, because 'white' ideas of God have been inculcated in association with another name, The-Chief-Above.... Some Masset people once fell to comparing The-Chief-Above with Power-of-the-Shining-Heavens in my presence. They said they were not the same." John R. Swanton, *Contributions to the Ethnology of the Haida*, Memoirs of the American Museum of Natural History, Volume VIII. Reprint from V, Part 1, of the Jessup North Pacific Expedition. Franz Boas, ed. (Leiden: E.J. Brill / New York: G.E. Stechert, 1905), pp. 13–14.

133 The Catholic church, now a private residence, was diagonally across the street from Fred's shop, on the corner of Delkatla and Collison Streets, New Masset.

134 The premium quality and quantity of wood from the Sitka spruce on Haida Gwaii, with its high strength to weight ratio, was in demand during World War I to build aircraft. The demand grew during World War II for building the de Havilland mosquito fighter-bombers, a twin-engine, two-seat bomber, made of wood and glue, famous for its light weight and superior handling.

135 "The largest log barge in the world operates in Masset Inlet and Masset Sound. The self-propelled and self-dumping barge, the *Haida Monarch*, is 129 metres (423 ft.) long and 26 meters (85 feet) wide, and can transport 15,000 tons of felled trees per load—equal to the contents of 400 logging trucks, or 12,000 telephone poles.... The smaller *Haida Brave* is 121 metres (397 ft.) long and 25 metres (82 ft.) wide, with a load capacity of 10,000 tons." Log barge: Port Clements BC, Haida Gwaii (Queen Charlotte Islands), as described at www.britishcolumbia.com/plan-your-trip/regions-and-towns/northern-bc-and-haida-gwaii/masset-inlet/.

Selected Bibliography

Abrahams, Caroline. "Ḵiid Ḵiyaas," a story of the Golden Spruce. In *Yakoun: River of Life*, Massett: Council of the Haida Nation, 1990.

Barbeau, Marius. "Haida Carvers in Argillite." National Museum of Man, *Bulletin Number 139*, Anthropological Series Number 38, 1957. Facsimile edition, Ottawa, 1974.

Barbeau, Marius. "King-ego, Haida Carver." Marius Barbeau Collection, Canadian Museum of History, B-F-550.12.

Barbeau, Marius. "Informant Captain Andrew Brown." Haida Totems in General, Northwest Coast Files, Marius Barbeau Collection, Canadian Museum of History, B.B. 285.64.

Barbeau, Marius. "Information from Alfred Adams" Northwest Coast Files, Marius Barbeau Collection, Canadian Museum of History, B-F- 253.2.

Bellis, Andrew. "The Masset Band." Unpublished paper, History 353, Dr. Hendrickson, University of Victoria, 1992.

Blackman, Margaret B. *During My Time: Florence Edenshaw Davidson, A Haida Woman*. Seattle: University of Washington Press / Vancouver: Douglas & McIntyre, 1982.

Blackman, Margaret B. "Percy Brown." In *Tales from the Queen Charlotte Islands, Book 1*. Massett: Senior Citizens of the Queen Charlotte Islands, 1979.

Boelscher, Marianne. *The Curtain Within: Haida Social and Mythical Discourse*. Vancouver: UBC Press, 1988.

Chittenden, Newton H. *Exploration of the Queen Charlotte Islands*. 1884. Reprint, Vancouver: Gordon Soules Book Publishers, 1984.

Collison, William Henry. *In the Wake of the War Canoe*. 1915. Reprint, Charles Lillard, ed. Victoria: Sono Nis Press, 1981.

Collison, William Henry. Letter to Church Missionary Society, London, April 4, 1878. In *Argillite: Art of the Haida*, Leslie Drew and Douglas Wilson, North Vancouver: Hancock House Publishers, 1981.

Dalzell, Kathleen E. *The Queen Charlotte Islands, 1774–1966, Volume 1*. Terrace: C.M. Adam, 1968. Reprint, Prince Rupert: Cove Press, 1973.

Davies, Mrs. V.A. de B. "Interesting Reminiscences of Henry Edenshaw," written upon the death of Henry Edenshaw, *North British Columbia News*, an insert from the *Vancouver Province*, ca. 1935.

Deasy, Thomas. Letters, 1911–1913. Library and Archives Canada, Indian Affairs Record Group 10 (RG10 1661), Ottawa, Ontario.

Dorsey, George A. "A Cruise Among Haida and Tlingit Villages about Dixon's Entrance." In *The Ghostland People: A Documentary History of the Queen Charlotte Islands, 1859–1906*. Charles Lillard, ed. Victoria: Sono Nis Press, 1989. Originally published in *Appletons' Popular Science Monthly*, Volume 53 (June 1898), from a lecture at Field Columbian Museum, Chicago, November 6, 1897.

Drew, Leslie, and Douglas Wilson. *Argillite: Art of the Haida*. North Vancouver: Hancock House, 1980.

Du Vernet, F.H., Bishop of Caledonia. "Bishop Du Vernet's Visit to the Queen Charlotte Islands." In *North British Columbia News*, Volume 2, Number 15 (July 1913), pp. 35–36.

Enrico, John. "Draft on Names." Unpublished manuscript, Old Massett, Haida Gwaii, 1991.

Enrico, John. *Haida Dictionary: Skidegate, Masset and Alaskan Dialects, Volume 1*. Fairbanks: Alaska Native Language Center, University of Alaska, Fairbanks / Juneau: Sealaska Heritage Institute, 2005.

Enrico, John, and Wendy Bross Stuart. *Northern Haida Songs*. Studies in the Anthropology of North American Indians. Lincoln: University of Nebraska Press, 1996.

Jones, Douglas. "Douglas Jones Abroad, Chapter 11." *North British Columbia News* Volume IV, Number 17, January 1914, p. 3.

KnowBC Blog. "Where Mountains Meet the Sea: A Coastal History." Chapter Three, Part Five: "The Residential Schools." KnowBC.com, June 27, 2010. See: https://www.knowbc.com/Knowbc-Blog/Where-Mountains-Meet-The-Sea-A-Coastal-History.

Lachler, Jordan. *Dictionary of Alaskan Haida*. Juneau: Sealaska Heritage Institute, 2010.

Lillard, Charles. *Just East of Sundown: The Queen Charlotte Islands*. Victoria: TouchWood Editions, 1995.

MacDonald, George F. *Haida Monumental Art: Villages of the Queen Charlotte Islands*. Vancouver: UBC Press, 1983.

Mallory, A.R., Stipendiary Magistrate. Magistrates Court in Re the Cases William Mathews [*sic*], Jimmy Harris and John Geddes, April 6, 1935. The Court's finding: April 27, 1935, Port Clements.

McCullum, Hugh, and Karmel Taylor McCullum. *Caledonia: 100 Years Ahead*. Toronto: Anglican Book Centre, 1979.

Murdock, George Peter. *Rank and Potlatch Among the Haida*. Yale University Publications in Anthropology Number 13, 1936; reprinted by Human Relations Area Files Press, New Haven, 1970.

O'Reilly, Peter. O'Reilly to Superintendent General of Indian Affairs, October 24, 1882, RC10, Records of Indian Reserve Commission. Letter book (1882–84). V1275, Mf. B-1391, BCARS. In Charles Lillard, *Just East of Sundown: The Queen Charlotte Islands*. Victoria: TouchWood Editions, 1995, p.114–15.

Outram, D.M. "Notes From The Farthest West." In *North British Columbia News*, ca. July 1911.

Phillips, David. "Potatoes." In *Growing Food on the Queen Charlotte Islands*, ed. Jane Kinegal and Sam Simpson, Masset: Friends of the Library, 1986.

Phillips, Howard B. "Fred Bellis—An Unforgettable Character." In *Tales from the Queen Charlotte Islands, Book 2*. Masset: Regional Council, Senior Citizens of the Queen Charlotte Islands, 1982.

Phillips, Howard B. *The New Masset Community Club: A Bit of History 1936–1963*. Tlell: Fingerprints, 1986.

Price, Alfred E. "Good News from Massett." In *North British Columbia News*, Number 36, May 1917.

Sheldon, Charles. "The Elusive Caribou," *The Wilderness of the North Pacific Coast Islands*. London: T. Fisher Unwin / New York: Charles Scribner's Sons, 1912. In *The Ghostland People*, Charles Lillard, Victoria: Sono Nis Press, 1989.

Simpson, Sam L. "Adventures in the Crab Trade." In *Tales from the Queen Charlotte Islands, Book 2*. Masset: Regional Council, Senior Citizens of the Queen Charlotte Islands, 1982.

Special Committees of the Senate and House of Commons. Meeting in Joint Session to Inquire into the Claims of the Allied Indian Tribes of British Columbia, as set forth in their edition submitted to Parliament in June 1926, Session 1926–1927. Proceedings, Reports and the Evidence. Printed by Order of Parliament, Ottawa, 1927. Appendix No. 2.

Stearns, Mary Lee. *Haida Culture in Custody: The Masset Band*. Vancouver: Douglas & McIntyre, 1981.

St. John's Church Missionary Society. Marriage and Baptism Records. Anglican Church Synod office, Diocese of Caledonia, Prince Rupert, BC.

Swanson, Mary. Spellings and translations of X̱aad Kil (Haida language).

Swanton, John R. *Contributions to the Ethnology of the Haida*. Memoirs of the American Museum of Natural History, Volume VIII. Reprint from V, Part I, of the Jesup North Pacific Expedition. Franz Boas, ed. Leiden: E.J. Brill / New York: G.E. Stechert, 1905.

Swanton, John R. *Haida Texts—Masset Dialect*. Memoirs of the American Museum of Natural History, Volume XIV, Part II. Reprint from X, Part II, of the Jesup

North Pacific Expedition. Franz Boas, ed. Leiden: E.J. Brill / New York: G.E. Stechert, 1908.

Tennant, Paul. "The Indian Land Question in British Columbia," *Aboriginal Peoples and Politics*. Vancouver: UBC Press, 1990. Reprint, 1992.

Throman, Reverend F.P. "New Church At Massett Completed." *North British Columbia News*, Number 44, May 1921, p. 12.

Turney, Ruth. "The Mission Boats." In *Tales from the Queen Charlotte Islands, Book 2*, Masset: Regional Council, Senior Citizens of the Queen Charlotte Islands, 1982.

Unknown. "Hudson's Bay Company Post At Masset Queen Charlotte Islands 1869–1898." In *The Charlottes: A Journal of the Queen Charlotte Islands, Volume 2*. Skidegate: Queen Charlotte Islands Museum Society, 1973.

Wright, Robin. *Northern Haida Master Carvers*. Seattle: University of Washington Press / Vancouver: Douglas & McIntyre, 2001.